VICTORIANA

■ COLLECTORS' ■
STYLE GUIDES

VICTORIANA

RACHAEL FEILD

Macdonald Orbis

A *Macdonald Orbis* Book
© Macdonald & Co (Publishers) Ltd 1988
© Text Rachael Feild 1988
First published in Great Britain in 1988
by Macdonald & Co (Publishers) Ltd
London & Sydney

A member of Maxwell Pergamon Publishing Corporation plc

British Library Cataloguing in Publication Data

Feild, Rachael
  Victoriana.____(Collectors' style guides).
  1. English antiques, 1837–1901 – Buyers' guides
  I. Title II. Series
  745.1'0942

  ISBN 0-356-15856-X

Editors Sarah Chapman, Hazel Harrison **Art Editor** Clive Hayball **Additional material** Malcolm
Haslam **Photography** Susanna Price **Designer** Paul Cooper **Filmset** Tradespools Ltd **Printed
and bound in Italy** at New Interlitho S.P.A.

Macdonald & Co (Publishers) Ltd
Greater London House
Hampstead Road
London NW1 7QX

A C K N O W L E D G E M E N T S
The publishers would like to thank the following for their advice and assistance in the
preparation of this book:
Richard Breeze, London; Hastwell & Howard, London; Jeanette Hayhurst, London; McIntosh
of Stockcross, Newbury; The Singing Tree, London; Wakelin & Linfield, Petworth; Bearne's of
Torquay; Bonham's; Christie's; Phillips; and Sotheby's.

Picture credits for the Introduction
p. 6 Mary Evans Picture Library; p. 8, 9 & 10 Christie's; p. 11 Phillips; p. 12 (left) Phillips, (right)
Mary Evans Picture Library; p. 13 Bridgeman Art Library; p. 15 Phillips; p. 16 Mansell
Collection; p. 18 & 19 Bridgeman Art Library.

Author's note on the Price Lists
The price lists are based on auction prices recorded during the last two years in European and
American salerooms. For the purposes of the list £1 = $1.90.
The price band given is only a guide. If an item is found which is priced below the lower price
given, collectors should make sure that it is genuine, and not damaged or restored. If, on the
other hand, the price being asked is higher than the top price given in the list, collectors should
ask themselves if the object is of particularly fine quality, particularly large of its sort, very rare,
or has some other exceptional feature.
The figure indicating quality of design and/or decoration is largely subjective, and the collector
will no doubt find it entertaining to compare his/her own taste with the author's.

CONTENTS

INTRODUCTION

'I had a little nut tree', coloured woodblock illustration by Walter Crane from *The Baby's Opera*, published in 1877.

'We may not be more moral, more imaginative, nor better educated than our ancestors', wrote John Hollingshead in the illustrated catalogue for the Decorative Arts Exhibition in 1862, 'but we have steam, gas, railways, and power-looms, while there are more of us, and we have more money to spend.'

This was the dilemma of a period which was more passionately concerned with art and design than any that had gone before. What is more, machines were uncontrollable in the face of such an unprecedented opportunity for the new industrialists to make themselves a fortune. The new entrepreneurs hung on every word written, printed or spoken, in every journal, magazine and lecture which concerned itself with 'taste', and reproduced as quickly as possible and in as much quantity what they interpreted those words to mean. The same symptoms were common in France and Italy, where the decadence of mass production imposed itself, twisting pure forms into tangles of plagiarism. Germany and Austria fared little better in their interpretations and revivals for the mass market. America, whose culture was still rooted in Europe, budded and bloomed with the nineteenth-century passion for ornament and ostentation, in all the mish-mash of styles that is collected or dismissed as 'Victoriana'.

THE RESTLESS END OF REGENCY

It was perhaps an unfortunate coincidence that in the same year that Victoria, a fair-haired girl of eighteen, was woken early on the morning of 20 June 1837 to the news that she was the Queen of England, the great disciplinarian of design and architecture, Sir John Soane, died. But the restlessness and desire for change had already begun and the experimentalists, the seekers after new sensations, new viewpoints, had already been at work for several decades.

'Novelty has a vast effect in archt'r', wrote Charles Cockerell in 1823, betraying in his writing a desire to speed things up, to communicate with breathless urgency. 'We are sick to see the same thing repeated over and over again what has been seen anytime these 100 yrs.' As early as 1805 he had designed the incongruous Mughal palace at Sezincote, with its bright-green copper domes obtruding on the soft Gloucestershire hills. And indeed, it was none other than that architect of sleek, neo-Georgian buildings, John Nash, who was responsible for the improbable Indian palace at Brighton, which lurked on the grey pebbled shores of Sussex like a beached sea-dragon. After almost a century of constricting good taste, people had begun to tire of the gracefully regimented façades of Georgian terraces, the classical proportions of Palladian houses, and the Chippendale and Hepplewhite furniture that furnished them.

The responsibility for these new flights of fancy has frequently been laid at Horace Walpole's door, and his Strawberry Hill has been singled out as the starting point for the Gothic revival in England. But Walpole's house was a singular folly, and 1750 was too far back in history to have had such a major and decisive role. Strawberry Hill grew around the core of an older romantic ruin, and on those grounds alone can be absolved. Fonthill Abbey, on the other

**Regency rosewood table with
ormolu mounts.**

hand, conceived by the eccentric William Beckford with the architect of Carlton House, James Wyatt, in 1796, rose as a testament to the power and skill of man, its 55m (180 ft) tower deliberately rivalling that of Salisbury Cathedral, with enough corbels, gargoyles and pinnacles to outshine anything built since the thirteenth century – or so William Beckford believed.

THE NEW AGE OF CHIVALRY

In 1825 young Augustus Pugin was given his first commission for furniture 'in the Gothic style', for Windsor Castle. Pugin was a scant fifteen years old at the time, but it was he who consolidated the 'new medievalism' in England. In France, one of

the most influential architects and designers of his century, Viollet-le-Duc, was treading the same path, restoring the Gothic heritage of France and designing stained glass for the Royal Chapel at Dreux and Amboise in the early 1840s.

When the old Houses of Parliament in London were totally destroyed by fire in 1834, it seemed only natural that a Gothic style should be chosen for the new building, which was duly designed by Charles Barry and begun in 1840. With the young Queen of England obviously so much in love with her handsome Consort, what could be more natural for this new age of chivalry than to choose the theme of the Arthurian Legends, the romance of Lancelot and Guinevere, embedded in the myths of centuries before? Augustus Pugin was wholly responsible for the interior design – the breathtaking gilded masonry, the giant murals, the Gothic tapestries and furnishings, even the umbrella stands and doorknobs – for the seat of the Mother of Parliaments.

During the reconstruction of the Houses of Parliament, Charles Eastlake, the leading architect-designer of his day, organized an exhibition of cartoons and drawings of the building, which was held in Westminster Hall, miraculously untouched by the fire. He was quite astonished at the response. 'I abridged the Catalogue to a penny size for the millions', he wrote, 'but many of the most wretchedly dressed people prefer the sixpenny one with the quotations...' 'All the workmen of the House of Parliament go in, but chiefly in the evening, because, being white as millers, they have themselves the discretion to time their visit.' This, surely, he thought, proved 'the love of the lower orders for pictures.'

The workmen, 'white as millers' from sanding down Portland stone, were in the very closest contact with Augustus Pugin's grand medieval design and the great romance of Arthur, Lancelot and Guinevere, and clearly the style appealed to the masses. In 1847, *Punch* commented that if cultures were to be judged by posterity in terms of their monuments and works of art 'we shall be treated as people who live in the middle ages, for everything around us partakes of the medieval character.'

IN SEARCH OF A BRITISH EMPIRE STYLE

As their Empire grew, the British began to search for a style to match its greatness, and what should be more natural than borrowing *le style Empire* from France, Europe's traditional leader of taste and fashion? So the Victorian era dawned to softly curving lines, pale colours, abundant gildings, rococo shapes and imitation plaster-moulded ceilings, very much in the grand manner. The style mixed well with the architecture of the time, and was impressive, rounded and comfortable. Pale grey or green ceilings and walls panelled with watered silk in gilded rococo surrounds do not immediately conjure up the spirit of 'Victoriana'. Yet most of the tasteful houses of the 1840s were light and airy, filled with cambric, lawn and printed cottons, with neat roller blinds, painted or printed, to keep the sun from fading the already pale colours of the spacious, neo-classical

Mid-Victorian oak library table.

Walnut settee in the rococo taste, about 1860.

interiors that were typical of the first years of Queen Victoria's reign.

Prince Albert had a most serious attitude towards both art and architecture, as well as design. Tentatively at first, and then with a surer hand and the able advice of Henry Cole, he began to guide such institutions as already existed, and to encourage them to lead style, taste and fashion. Henry Cole was a shining light in the field of art manufacture, and first came to Prince Albert's attention because of a tea service he had designed for Herbert Minton. In 1847 the Royal Society for the Encouragement of Arts, Manufactures and Commerce staged its first exhibition, organized by Henry Cole. The catalogue made quite plain the intentions of the event:

'It is a universal complaint among manufacturers that the taste for good Art does not exist in sufficient extent to reward them for the cost of producing superior works; that the people prefer the vulgar, the gaudy, the ugly even, to the beautiful and perfect. We are persuaded that if Artistic Manufactures are not appreciated, it is because they are not widely enough known. We believe that when works of high merit, of British origin, are brought forward, they will be fully appreciated and thoroughly enjoyed. We believe that this exhibition when thrown open gratuitously to all, will tend to im-

Mid-Victorian 'sociable', covered with a cotton print.

prove the public taste.' It is likely, however, that public taste was more gratified by an exhibition of Ancient and Medieval Decorative Art, which was put on three years later by Henry Cole, in 1850.

Charles Eastlake thought that public taste had already improved by the time that the Great Exhibition was launched in 1851. 'People began to discover', he noted with pleasure, 'that the round bulbous form of decanter was a more pleasant object to look at than the rigid outline of a pseudo-crystal pint pot carved and chopped about into unnecessary grooves and planes. The reversed and truncated cone, which served our grandfathers for wine glasses, gradually disappeared before the lily and crocus shaped bowls from which we now sip our sherry and Bordeaux. Champagne has formerly been drunk from tall and narrow glasses...it is now a broad and shallow tazza which sparkles with the vintage of Epernay.' So it was out with the tall and elegant flute glass and in with the impractical shallow bowl on a stalk; and that word 'bulbous' was an ominous foretaste of the styles that were to come.

Peacock by Minton's, modelled by Paul Comolera.

TASTE AND THE CRYSTAL PALACE

The Prince Consort, who did not know the English nor their culture very well, was greatly encouraged by the Royal Society's exhibition in 1847, and ambitious plans were set afoot for the Great Exhibition. This exhibition is still considered as the dividing line in the long period that produced 'Victoriana', though quite incorrectly. Prince Albert remarked thoughtfully that 'there are two great auxiliaries in this country which seldom fail to promote the success of any scheme – fashion and a high example... Fashion we know is all in all in England, and if the Court – I mean the Queen and myself – set the example hereafter by having works of this kind done [in this case he was talking about frescoes] the same taste will extend itself to worthy individuals. The English country seats, which are the most beautiful in the world, would acquire additional effect from the introduction of such a style of decoration, and with such occupation the school would never languish and would at least have time to develop itself fully.' Alas for the   11

Stoneware garden seat made about 1890 by Doulton's of Lambeth.

English seats, many of them were torn down to make way for more fashionable, but oppressive, high-ceilinged, cathedral-like buildings suitable for murals, frescoes, stained glass and the like.

Of the two court principals it was Prince Albert who had the better taste, and he died in 1861. Some indication of Victoria's taste is given in a note in her Journal for 12 July 1851. On her visit to the Great Exhibition, she wrote: 'The taste of some of the plate and jewellery is beautiful; none struck us so much, as likely to be useful for the taste of the country, as Elkington's beautiful specimens of electro-plate.' Elkington's principal exhibit was a 1.2 m (4 ft) high vase on a square-mounted pedestal, crowned by a statuette of Victoria's beloved Albert. It was called *The Triumph of Science* and

was designed and modelled by William Beattie, with four statuettes at each corner: one of Newton, for Astronomy; one of Shakespeare, for Poetry; one of Bacon, for Philosophy; and one of James Watt, for Mechanics (who must seldom have found himself in such august company).

In terms of aesthetic achievement, the Great Exhibition was on the whole classified as a dismal failure. Letters to *The Times* attacked 'the sins committed against good taste' and the 'vulgarities of our manufactures'. The editor of the *Journal of Design and Manufactures* com-

The Albert Memorial, from an engraving, 1872.

plained bitterly of the lack of discipline in ornamental design, and angrily penned his opinion that 'the mass of ornament applied to the works ... exhibited ... was meretricious'. Similarly, R. N. Wornum's

The Monarch of the Glen by Sir Edwin Landseer.

essay entitled *The Exhibition as a Lesson in Taste* stated that 'the taste of the producers in general' was 'uneducated'. Henry Cole and his followers were less impressed by the designs or their display than by the speed of their manufacture, which was quite remarkable.

It was not only in England, though, that there was a general decline in taste and design. All over Europe, poor reproductions of earlier shapes and forms filled salons, dining and reception rooms in a style called *tous les Louis* or, more unkindly, *Louis le hôtel*. In Paris, many of the most

gifted and talented designers and architects refused to study at the Ecole des Beaux Arts, which they despised. Only in Germany was something genuinely new emerging. Born out of the great impoverishment that followed the Napoleonic wars, coupled with a dislike for all things French, the Biedermeier style sounded a note of relative sanity in a world cluttered with ornament and frills.

In 1854, after almost forty years of peace, prosperity and a rising population, England went to war in the Crimea, fighting side by side with France against the Turk. At home, 13

442,000 labourers worked on the building sites of terraces, avenues and crescents of houses for the growing numbers of families, and more than one-and-a-half million textile workers were employed to make curtains and drapes to furnish these houses and for export to the colonies. It was not only her manufactured goods that Britain sent abroad in the mid-nineteenth century. In 1850 there were over one-and-a-quarter million people born in Britain living in America – in 1860 the numbers had risen to nearly two-and-a-quarter million. In 1858 the Princess Royal, Queen Victoria's eldest daughter, married Prince Frederick of Prussia, and French opinion turned against the British – a sentiment which was reciprocated. And so, instead of the *le style Empire*, the plain, utilitarian furniture from Germany, designed mainly by craftsmen and christened 'Biedermeier', became acceptable in England.

In 1851 Sir Charles Phipps, secretary to the Prince Consort, had expressed the aims of the Great Exhibition. 'The object', he wrote, 'must not be so much the founding of institutions through which Great Britain may be raised to an equality, or maintain her stature over other nations, as the foundation of some establishment in which by the application of science and art to industry proceeds, the industry of all nations may be raised in the scale of human employment; and where, by the constant interchange of ideas, experience and its results, each nation may gain and contribute something. There is no doubt that in such an interchange England would ultimately be the great gainer.' It must be said that England had already 'borrowed' ideas from almost everywhere, the latest

culture being the Ottoman Empire, which the British had recently encountered in the Crimea.

Fashion, however, is not the sole arbiter of taste, and in 1859 an event of earth-shaking significance to the English-speaking world occurred, which ensured a continued and emotional attachment to Gothic, Medieval and ecclesiastical styles. *The Origin of Species* by Charles Darwin threw the civilized world into confusion, reinforced church attendance, elevated the curate as the new star of mawkish, moralizing fiction and strengthened Victorian moral attitudes. Every bedroom had its prie-dieu, every household its morning prayers. Procreation was regarded as clearly bestial, though essential. It was pure coincidence that the crinoline arrived the same year, caging women in iron hoops and swathing them in layers of concealing skirts. With great ingenuity, the Empress Eugénie, wife of Napoleon III, had launched the fashion to aid the depressed textile industry in France, undercut by cheap imports of silk from the East.

GREENERY YALLERY AND WRENAISSANCE

Across the Atlantic, in 1854, America dragged Japan out of her fourteenth-century isolationism and into the world of commerce, causing one of the greatest untapped reservoirs of influence to flood the Western world at the beginning of the 1860s. In England, the 'Anglo-Japanese' style was seized upon by a group of beautiful young men who considered themselves to be as much above the world of vulgar commerce as they were above the apes. Inspired by the books of Walter Pater, they dubbed them-

14

Watercolour painted in 1887 by William Stephen Coleman.

selves 'Aesthetes' and soon collected a devoted following of artists, writers and designers. They painted their ceilings celadon green and their walls in muddy shades of yellow and won themselves the nickname of 'the greenery-yallery set'. Their rooms were furnished with Japanese screens and insubstantial furniture, a great deal of it in ebonized wood fashioned into elegant spindles, bobbins and balusters, and decorated with flowers, artistic painting and discreet gilding.

It was a very small group, with very little influence at the time, because, simultaneously in the 1870s, there was a general swing back to what the Victorians considered to be the 'Queen Anne' style. In essence, this consisted of houses built in red brick, often with a liberal addition of 'Jacobean' beams and timbering, with 'Adam'-style interiors mixed with a dash of Japanese. Everything had to be new, nothing genuinely old, al-

though fake Elizabethan was acceptable. Panels were ripped from early churches to make coffers and linen presses and to cover the walls of so-called, but misconceived, 'Queen Anne' interiors. Meanwhile, other eager architects were filling the desecrated churches with 'Gothic' rood screens and 'Renaissance' altars.

And still the dichotomy of man versus machine tore at the moral attitudes of the high priests of design. Walter Crane, one of the sternest critics of industrial production, gave a lecture during this period to the students of art at Armstrong College, Newcastle-upon-Tyne. 'As to Machinery', he said, 'I do not deny that it has its uses or that wonderful (and sometimes fearful) things have been produced; the commercial output is prodigious, in fact, modern existence has come to depend upon machinery in nearly every direction, but the machines themselves remain as a rule far more

'Aesthetic' interior of about 1875.

wonderful things than they produce, and the less machinery has to do with Art the better.' Yet by the end of the 1870s, a 'Queen Anne' house was liable to have a Walter Crane frieze in the drawing room, and Walter Crane tiles and wallpapers throughout the house, as well as Walter Crane books in the nursery – all mass-produced by machines.

FURNISHING 'IN THE ANTIQUE'

Impossible then, to ignore machines and machinery. There was surely only one thing to do, and that was to make them work the way Man wanted, without degrading every idea and style they were offered, which had largely been the case up till now. Without a doubt the lead came from the United States of America. Lately recovered from an almost suicidal Civil War, which lasted from 1861 to 1865, and hungry for domestic goods of every kind, America was in the grip of 'Centennial mania' as it celebrated its first hundred years of independence in 1876. Every home had to have its Shaker sewing chair, its own homebred arts and crafts. By the 1880s the manufacture of reproduction antique furniture was an industry of some size.

Meanwhile, England struggled with the twin forces of heritage and wealth. The 'Queen Anne' style had demanded that everything should be in matching sets – glasses, porcelain, china, chair covers, curtains and dining chairs, pier glasses, console tables, side tables and mirrors. But towards the end of the 1870s there was a move away from this symmetry, led by the architects and designers of the Aesthetic Movement. The first conscious efforts at furnishing 'in the antique' were made, with

results that were generally known as 'shabby genteel'. Reproductions *per se* were frowned on, though furniture-making companies such as Gillows continued to make 'Chippendale' mahogany furniture, which they had done without a break ever since the *Director* was first published in 1754. And so the fashionable furnished their interiors with 'antique' but painted it white, lacquer red or dark green.

An even better compromise was found for the new blocks of apartments that were springing up all over London and the principal cities in the provinces – a little bit of everything was the rule. 'The ante-chamber should be Gothic or Renaissance, the salon or drawing room in the Louis style with card tables and rococo curves. The dining room should be Gothic, Renaissance, or in the French style of Henry II or Louis XIV with carved black oak furniture, stained-glass windows, faience plates hanging on the walls and big garnitures on the mantelshelf.' (Thus wrote architect-author Ris-Paquot in 1890, echoing a scheme of things that had been worked out in London in the 1870s.) Bedrooms somehow were always thought to be 'French' and 'they should be furnished with rosewood, marquetry, satinwood, or maple with Sèvres plaques.' These rules were, for a time, followed in America where, after Mr. Elisha Otis invented the 'safety elevator' in 1852, the number of apartments increased.

THE HEIGHT OF CLUTTER

In the cluttered rooms of the late 1870s and 1880s, furniture was arranged in dense islands on either side of passages, like well-worn rabbit runs, so that the ladies could

William Powell Frith: *The Railway Station*, painted in 1862.

move about without sweeping a cargo of treasure off an occasional table, or even capsizing an entire whatnot with one injudicious swing of their skirts. The shape of furniture changed to accommodate the billowing structure of female dress, sinking lower and becoming rounder, with less and less well-defined silhouettes. The ottomans and divans of Turkey, the unsupported, sprawling shapes of the East, invaded the drawing room from the decent privacy of smoking rooms where they had first spread themselves after the Crimean War. Generations of unmarried women, born in the long and fertile years of peace at the beginning of Victoria's reign, stitched and sewed away at chair and seat covers, smoking caps, slippers and antimacassars, in woolwork, beadwork and silk. Everywhere, everything had exceeded even the most gloomy predictions of undisciplined taste.

William Morris was scathing about the overblown roses embroidered and woven into carpets, printed over loose covers and climbing up the curtains and drapes. In his hands, the acanthus, the anthemion, the lily, the pomegranate and the rose

became swirling two-dimensional patterns in sombre greens, blues and yellow ochres. What was new was Morris's approach to surface design, which could be repeated by machine on paper or textile without suffering distortion or debasement.

Today, the name of William Morris is sometimes bracketed with Art Nouveau, but in fact he was far more closely allied with the Arts and Crafts Movement, together with Walter Crane, who was instrumental in founding the Arts and Crafts Exhibition Society. William Morris was not a Pre-Raphaelite in terms of artistic style, even though the Pre-Raphaelite protagonists, Burne-Jones, Rossetti, Ford Madox Brown and Philip Webb were among those with whom he established the firm, Morris, Marshall, Faulkner & Co. The company's aim was to promote well-designed domestic furniture and furnishings, and at the International Exhibition of 1862 it filled two stands with its exhibits, which included the famous St. George cabinet, designed by Webb and painted by Morris. Most of the early production of Morris & Co., as the company shortly became, consisted of stained glass.

GOOD TASTE ON THE SURFACE

The main influence that William Morris exerted over interior design at the end of the century was almost entirely in surface decoration of one kind or another – wallpapers, textiles, carpets, friezes, tapestries, and painted decoration – and in all of this the recognizably sinuous lines of the Art Nouveau style are forcefully apparent. Without a doubt he made a major contribution to the grand renaissance in decorative art that swept Europe in the last decade of the nineteenth century.

But Morris's style was certainly not the only influential one at the time. His sombre colours and stern *fin de siècle* discipline were a far cry from the 'Naughty Nineties', with its totally frivolous, joyous bad taste.

Like children educated in convents and seminaries, the last generation of the nineteenth century burst on the world in frills and ostrich feathers, embroidered silk waistcoats and loudly checked tweeds. And when the ageing Queen, beloved of all, seated herself in the Telegraph Room at Buckingham Palace on the morning of 22 June 1897, to transmit her Diamond Jubilee message to her multi-racial subjects, even she at last had tired of her mourning attire. She wore a dress of black moiré, true, but it was panelled in dove grey and embroidered all over with silver shamrocks, roses and thistles. It is a wonder, in all the clamour and excitement, that the small cries of protest from John Ruskin, William Morris and their earnest disciples were heard at all.

Dancing at the Moulin Rouge by Toulouse-Lautrec.

19

CHAPTER   ONE

FURNITURE

Leather-upholstered desk chair
Height: 86 cm
Richard Breeze, London
Price: £440

The difference between the eighteenth century and the nineteenth in furniture-making was that where there had been pattern books, now there were catalogues. Ever since the publication of Chippendale's *The Gentleman and Cabinet Maker's Director* in 1754, designers of furniture had followed his successful lead and produced pattern books of furniture and furnishings for the rich and the not-so-rich. The firm of Chippendale and Rannie built and supplied all the furniture and fabrics illustrated in the *Director*. Messrs. Ince and Mayhew, one of the largest rivals in the field, also had furniture workshops where their designs were made to the highest standards. But other design and pattern books were printed principally for cabinet-makers in the provinces, so that they could follow London fashions and themselves make furniture 'in the

style of' the most desirable designers of the day.

As early as 1767, Richard Gillow of Lancaster was writing to a client with the object of taking liberties with Chippendale's designs. To a couple of his own sketches for proposed library bookcases he pinned a note saying: 'If any of Chippendale's designs be more agreeable I have his book and can execute 'em and adapt them to the places they are for if you'll be so obliging as to point out the number.' There were guilds and societies to protect designers and prevent pirating, but by the end of the eighteenth century no power on earth could arrest the great juggernaut of demand which followed such publications as *Household Furniture in Genteel Taste* and *The Chair Maker's Guide... with 200 new and genteel designs*. The term 'genteel' itself drew the sharp comment that it simply meant anything with a rounded, curved or comfortable shape.

TASTE AND TERRACED HOUSES

While gentlemen continued to meet and discuss the design, furniture and furnishings of their huge new houses, the multiplying rows of terraced houses rose on land belonging to the great estates, and interior design was left to the speculative builder or to the families who rented from him. Furniture was cast loose from its architectural moorings to float on a sea of ready-made, relatively well-produced and easily marketable designs, laid out in catalogues illustrating every conceivable design, many of them pirated from the new edition of Chippendale's *Director* which was reissued in 1834.

Le style crapaud, as early horsehair button-backed upholstered chairs, settees and stools were nicknamed by the French who originated them, were among the early 'rococo revival' or 'French Empire' furnishings to be made for a multitude of houses, whose numbers grew as the population expanded inexorably in the long years of peace and Empire-building between the resounding victory of Waterloo in 1815 and the fiasco of the Crimean War in 1854. But even this style, the curves and comfort of which appealed to the new generations of the middle class, soon overflowed its disciplined lines. In

1828 Samuel Pratt patented the coiled metal spring for upholstered seat furniture, and the controlled curves of horsehair upholstery blossomed into more buxom, deeply dimpled shapes.

New techniques also began to change the ways of the craftsmen. Steam-driven machines cut marble for console tables and chiffoniers, turned bobbins and twisted barley sugar uprights. The straight-legged classical Regency chairs thickened and coarsened with bulbous 'classical' shapes. New methods of steaming timber to bend and shape it, together with the contemporary pas-

Balloon-back chair
Height: 82.2 cm
Richard Breeze, London
Price (pair): £280

23

sion for curves, brought rounded chair-frames, their backs panelled with upholstery at first, then with machine-carved ornamental open backs. Known at first as 'corset backs' these were the early versions of the ubiquitous balloon back which is so characteristic of the period.

Davenport
Height: 88.9 cm
Richard Breeze, London
Price: £880

Machine-cut veneers laid over cheap deal, imported pine or other softwoods could at first glance look little different from expensive cabinet-maker's work. With the addition of French polishing, no piece of furniture could possibly have been mistaken for 'old'; everything was shiny, bobbined, swashturned and veneered. And where once the bare essentials were all that was needed for comfortable living, now there had to be all manner of extra decorative pieces to hold massive lamps, plant pots, jardinières and statuary.

By mid-century London covered

Jardinière with Minton tiles inset
Height: 43.2 cm
Richard Breeze, London
Price: £185

Piano stool
Height: 46 cm
Sold: Christie's, Great Tew Park,
28/5/87
Price: £374

about 316 sq km (122 square miles), and the surrounding orchards, meadows and market gardens disappeared under more and more houses. The population had increased from less than two million at the beginning of the century to more than three-and-a-half million, living in 400,778 houses arranged in more than 10,500 terraces, squares, crescents and streets. As a contemporary guide book noted, London had acquired 'the Northern suburbs' of Kensington and Bayswater, and 'over the water', the southern suburbs of Battersea, Clapham and Wandsworth. 'Taking the population of the four counties in which London stands, we shall arrive at a number above four million – a population perfectly Chinese in its density', wrote a contributor to *Routledge's Popular Guide to London and its Suburbs* in 1871. Three-quarters had an average annual income of £300. £500 a year was a respectable income for a young middle-class couple setting up house, but as the writer was at pains to observe, 'a glance at the palatial mansions in the suburbs, particularly Brompton, Kensington, St. John's Wood, Bayswater and Hampstead' belied this rather modest financial statistic. Nor did he mention the appalling poverty of the spreading slums.

Unguided, the taste of the growing

Painted cupboard in neo-Gothic style
Height: 172.7 cm
Richard Breeze, London
Price: £595

wealthy middle classes was uncultivated and to a large extent, undiscriminating. J. C. Loudon's *Encyclopaedia of Cottage, Farm and Villa Architecture and Furniture*, published in 1833, attempted to guide the choice of the fashionable Gothic revival designs that were thought to be suitable for those gingerbread follies that can still be seen nestling in the most unlikely parts of the country – the *cottages ornés* of the turn of the century. In these, and little gazebos in the garden, the contemporary delight in the rustic and romantic was given full play with great exuberance, and all were furnished in the quaint taste of their owners. Loudon, the hand that guided, did not foresee that the designs for this furniture destined for these rural *pieds à terre* would find their way into town houses, but they inevitably did.

STRAIGHT BACKS AND GOTHIC MORALITY

In the 1850s and 1860s a style loosely derived from the designs of Pugin and Burges, but far more generally an outright robbing from early Tudor and Jacobean periods, began to supplant the rounded, comfortable forms of the early Victorian era. It was as though, along with their morals, people had straightened their backs to accord with their stiff-necked attitude to life. Artificially seasoned oak played a large part in

Pair of pole-screens
Height: 142.2 cm
Richard Breeze, London
Price: £950

the recreation of 'Tudorbethan' styles. Apart from brand new copies of traditional panel-backed chairs and settles, there was a rediscovery of genuinely old pieces of furniture, such as buffets and Welsh dressers, aumbries, linen presses and immensely heavy oak coffers and chests, strapped with iron and weighed down with locks of steel.

The neo-Gothic trend was given a huge boost by the Medieval Court at the exhibition of 1851. Morris, Marshall, Faulkner & Co., during the firm's early years, was mainly concerned with the manufacture of stained glass for the ecclesiastical and domestic market, which was an aspect of the prevailing taste for neo-Gothic. There was a demand for 27

**Papier-mâché chair inlaid with
mother-of-pearl**
Height: 80.6 cm
Sold: Christie's East, New York,
16/12/86
Price: $605

stained glass not only for the multitude of churches in which the inhabitants of the new suburbs could worship regularly, but also for the great oak-beamed entrance halls, billiard rooms, smoking rooms and libraries of the newly arrived gentry. Charles Eastlake's *Hints on Household Taste*, which was first published as a series of articles in the *Queen* magazine in 1865, reinforced the fashion for Gothic-style furniture, with chip-carved panels, arches and balusters; and the architect and designer Bruce Talbert actually played into the hands of the mass-producers by designing a simplified version of geometric Gothic.

Machine-carving turned out acres of 'linenfold' panelling for halls, dining rooms and reception rooms. Gothic traceries and fretwork were accomplished in a matter of hours with steam-powered saws and planes. While J. G. Crace & Sons made very fine furniture for Pugin, Burges and Godwin, and Jackson & Graham executed many of Eastlake's original designs, plagiarism was rife, and dozens of manufacturers cashed in with poorly made travesties of far loftier designs. One company, C. & R. Light of Shoreditch, was singled out for condemnation by C. R. Ashbee who called its products 'slaughtered furniture'.

Gillows, still very much in business after several generations, forsook work in the traditional manner in order to compete with other firms exhibiting at the Great Exhibition of 1851, clearly to their detriment. *The Illustrated London News* was disparaging: 'The Library Table, Sofa and Easy chair ... are specimens of the more substantial class of furniture, in which it has been attempted to combine extreme solidity with elaborate adornment. We confess we are by no means well pleased with the result.' The accompanying illustration shows a wildly extravagant design, with a sofa supported with gryphons whose wings are spread in shell-like contours to support the curved sides, while beneath the upholstered seat a riotous swirl of carved foliage and flowers seems to prance from one end to the other.

It was a style that was never given house-room in the average drawing rooms of even the largest terraced house. The severe, geometrical lines of furniture designed by Bruce Talbert and made by Thomas Seddon of New Bond Street were a welcome antidote to the overblown French rococo style. The firm, which moved to South Molton Street, made furniture with traditional tongue-and-groove construction, pegging, and good solid craftsmanship. Some of this furniture was exhibited in the Great Exhibition's Medieval Court, side by side with designs by Pugin for furniture made by J. G. Crace. But it was at the International Exhibition of 1862 that Thomas Seddon's son, John Pollard Seddon, caught the imagination of the public, and this led to a plethora of cheaper versions of his work.

AMERICAN STYLE

American design was late to slide into the morass of mixed taste and style. Top cabinet-makers in Boston, New York and Philadelphia made fine neo-classical and taper-legged Regency furniture based on the pattern books of Thomas Sheraton in the early nineteenth century. One of its principal exponents, Duncan Phyfe, was still working in the 1840s in the same style, and the Biedermeier influence was adopted much sooner across the Atlantic than in England. But by the middle of the nineteenth century a rococo revival was underway, curiously sinuous and quite different from any other. It was centred in New York, where German cabinet-makers and craftsmen far outnumbered those of any other extraction, and was led by Henry Belter, who came to America from Württemburg in 1844.

Henry Belter was a technician as well as a craftsman, and he developed a new form of laminated wood which could not only be steamed and bent into serpentine and curved shapes, but could also be pierced and carved. He worked principally in rosewood, a heavy timber from Brazil with a redder colour than mahogany, streaked with black. The ornate, carved and curving style of his work was soon taken up by furniture-makers in Boston and Philadelphia. The height of this rococo revival period is at its most extravagant in the *étagères* (an overgrown cross between a whatnot and a chiffonier) which dominated the parlours of the rich and fashionable. The overall design was in fact not very far from the maligned *Louis le hôtel*, current on the other side of the Atlantic.

In wholesome contrast, a vogue was growing for rough-hewn, rugged furniture, which was being made

Papier-mâché chair inlaid with mother-of-pearl
Height: 82.8 cm
Sold: Christie's East, New York,
16/12/86
Price: $660

from necessity by the frontiersmen of the West. When Charles Eastlake's *Hints on Household Taste* was published in London in 1868, advocating the use of plain, solid wood decorated with chip-carving and archi-

traves, Americans made his book their Bible. The Eastlake style was adopted and plagiarized to such an extent that Eastlake himself issued a severe admonishment in the fourth edition of his book, published in 1878. He found, he said, 'American tradesmen continually advertising what they are pleased to call 'Eastlake' furniture, with the production of which I have had nothing whatever to do, and for the taste of which I should be very sorry to be considered responsible.'

Marble-topped pine washstand with tiles inset
Height: 102.8 cm
Richard Breeze, London
Price: £280

VOX POP AND THE QUEEN ANNE STYLE

With Prince Albert's death in 1862, and the end of the Empress Eugénie's influence on fashion and taste following the Franco-Prussian War of 1870–71, there was no figurehead to follow, no example set, in any part of the wide-ranging field of design. There were dozens of conflicting shapes and styles on the market, mostly made to standards which fulfilled price rather than craftsmanship, and all available from catalogues freely supplied by large furniture-making companies in London and the provinces. Partly from expediency, because it was cheaper to produce 'sets' and 'suites' of domestic furniture and furnishings, taste swung towards a rough approximation of 'Queen Anne', though many of the more avant-garde ladies then writing in books and magazines showed a rare contempt for the genuine article. 'One word may be advisable on the subject of the recent rage for 'Chippendale' and so-called 'Queen Anne' furniture,' wrote Mrs Haweis in *The Art of Beauty*, published in 1878. 'Let no one suppose that in furnishing with this kind of manufacture they are encouraging art, or supporting the Beautiful. The greater part of the objects which pass under the name of Queen Anne are (I speak of genuine old work), of course, not of the period of Queen Anne at all, but of the later Georges.

'Chippendale is the name of a conscientious manufacturer, at the beginning of the present century [she may have been certain of her opinions, but had a weak grasp of the facts] whose chief merit was that he possessed the now-extinct art of making joints that were strong, yet

Etagère **with inlaid decoration**
Height: 81.2 cm
Richard Breeze, London
Price: £495

delicate, and drawers that would open without shrieking, and without undue violence on the part of the puller.' This clearly demonstrates the miserable standards of manufacture at the time Mrs Haweis was writing. She continues firmly, '...beautiful his work was not, in the artistic sense, but only in a mechanical one. The heavy lyre-backed chairs with horse-hair seats, the fragile tables which seem to aim at having no legs – the straight diamond-paned bookcases of mahogany, with brazen-handled drawers – useful they may all be in their way – beautiful they never can be called.'

'The age of Queen Anne (1702–14) was an age equally celebrated for the absence of art, an absence so complete and so conscious, that no at-

31

Biedermeier dining chair
Height: 77.5 cm
Sold: Christie's, South Kensington,
London, 28/10/87
Price (set of 6): £935

the followers of Mrs. Haweis, who was only voicing the opinion of the majority. It is not difficult, however, to see that the Victorian balloon-backed chair was to a great extent derived from the 'buckle-backed' Biedermeier designs of the 1820s and 1830s. The loops and curves of Michael Thonet's bentwood furniture were, on the other hand, in complete harmony with popular taste, though too lightweight for an important place in the scheme of things.

SPOILT FOR CHOICE

Cassell's Household Guide, published in 1875, tried hard to steer its readers between the jagged reefs of too much choice. 'Suppose that our taste inclines us to admire ornament which consists chiefly of natural forms . . . like the Gothic artists of the decorated period, who introduced flowers, foliage, animals, and the human form, in every conceivable combination', runs an essay on 'The Principles of Good Taste in Household Furnishings'. 'Adopting this naturalism as our leading principle, we introduce natural forms throughout the enrichments.' The advice was to have tables with an 'animal crouching underneath', chairs with 'carved foliage or fruit on the legs and back; and the sofa . . . designed in the same spirit.' Here, too, is evidence of the rising trend of fashionable clutter. 'Some seem to think that you cannot have too much of a good thing, and that the more ornament you can introduce the better.'

tempt was made to break the monotony of straight lines, and, where there is no real creative ability, there is certainly some virtue in avoiding offence.' All of this goes to show that Victorian 'Queen Anne' was frequently distorted, always ornamented, and seldom faithfully reproduced, except in small things and in silver.

It was small wonder, too, that the simple lines of German Biedermeier furniture, stripped of ornament, plain and uncompromising, were not seized upon by the mass-producers of ready-made furniture, for they would not have been well received by

By the early 1880s clutter was at its height. The last two decades of 'Victoriana' are those which are taken as a model for the whole period – dark, gloomy rooms swathed in drapes, harsh gaslight showing up soot and dirt on a multitude of ornaments, no style, no grace, no feeling for design. There is a popular myth that the Victorians were so prudish that they covered the table legs so that they did not offend. The truth is more practical. Most provincially minded households wanted to show

Bed-step commode
Height: 48.3 cm
Richard Breeze, London
Price: £225

Bentwood coatstand
Height: 188 cm
Sold: Christie's, Great Tew Park,
28/5/87
Price: £528

off their financial stability and their standing in society with good, solid mahogany, with acres of highly polished surfaces to indicate a large staff of servants, and with plenty of statuary, porcelain, lace and needlework made by the mistress of the house. This was additional proof that she was a lady of leisure and never gave a hand with making beds or washing the silver and glass, which she almost certainly did. But French 33 polish marks almost instantly if a damp glass or a warm plate is placed on it, and beneath the floor-length embroidered table-covers the furniture was most probably old-fashioned, or extremely cheap. Heavy chenille with runners of hand-made point lace disguised everything beneath it, with the added advantage that all the ornaments could be lifted off, placed on a tray, and the table-cover shaken smartly out of the window to dislodge the dust and grime.

Oak armchair
Height: 87.2 cm
Sold: Phillips, London, 24/3/87
Price: £308

Ladies' writing desk in the 'Aesthetic' style
Height: 134.6 cm
Richard Breeze, London
Price: £575

NEW LIGHT AT THE END OF AN ERA

The harshness of gas lighting played an important role in sweeping away the dark drapes, the clutter and the stiflingly overloaded interiors of the last two decades of Queen Victoria's reign. It cast no sharp shadows, and was more akin to modern fluorescent light in its quality. Surface decoration was far more effective under this lighting than carving, and many of the furniture fashions that had been embraced by the upper echelons of society in the 1860s were found to be eminently suitable for the many households that were supplied with town gas from the 1870s, and even electricity in the last decade of the nineteenth century.

Among the most effective furniture under the flaring gasoliers was the black and gilt 'Japanesque', the design of which was pioneered by the architect E. W. Godwin and adopted by other designers. Some of the motifs designed by the Aesthetic Movement were also adapted for the mass market, but the designs are heavier.

Charles Voysey had done much to

strip away unnecessary ornament and, like his predecessor William Morris, return to simple shapes and forms. 'The intemperate indulgence in display and elaboration,' he wrote in 1894, 'and the feverish thirst for artificial excitement are all part and parcel of our proverbial restlessness. Too much luxury is the death of the artistic soul.' The simplicity of his furniture was cruelly dismissed as 'the rabbit hutch school', but in his hands it was far from such crude imagery, while in the hands of his imitators it sometimes was not.

Setting out to buy good pieces of Victorian furniture is a question of brinkmanship. Every decade has its high points and its low ones, and every manufacturer fell from grace at some moment, leaving what they were best at and trying to compete in the open market. Early pieces by Gillow in traditional styles are excellent – late innovative Gillow is even better. Mid-century Gillow lost its way, and it is better to look for middle-of-the-road names such as W. & A. Smee, William Watt, and good unmarked pieces by Jackson & Graham. Collinson & Lock may still be affordable, whereas J. G. Crace is out of the question. Holland & Sons are attainable and of a high quality, while the earlier firm, Holland & Co. is too expensive. During its long period in the wilderness, a great deal of Victorian furniture was broken up or, at the very least, badly neglected and knocked about. Because of its machine-made components, it has not been too difficult with the use of modern methods to match lost legs and table tops, to cannibalize twelve chairs into a convincing six, and so the buyer must always beware of the possibility of finding reconstituted pieces.

Mahogany dresser in the style of E. W. Godwin
Height: 184 cm
Sold: Phillips, London, 24/3/87
Price: £286

35

Object	Quality of manufacture	Quality of design and/or decoration	Rarity	Price (£)	Price ($)
Bookcases					
mahogany/walnut glazed	7	6	■ ■	400–700	760–1330
oak breakfront	7	7	■ ■	400–600	760–1140
mahogany bureau bookcase	8	7	■ ■ ■	700–1000+	1330-1900+
mahogany revolving bookcase	7	6	■ ■	400–700	760–1330
Cabinets					
satinwood display cabinet	8	6	■ ■	800–1000+	1520–1900+
fruitwood collector's cabinet	7	7	■ ■ ■	500–800	950–1520
ebonized wood side-cabinet	6	7	■	400–600	760–1140
mahogany chiffonier	7	6	■ ■	200–500	380–950
Chairs					
Biedemeier-style dining chairs (set of six)	7	7	■ ■	750–1000+	1425–1900+
oak armchair	7	6	■ ■	200–500	380–950
mahogany/walnut piano stool	7	7	■ ■	150–400	285–760
papier-mâché chair with mother-of-pearl inlay	7	7	■ ■	150–350	285–665
leather-upholstered desk chair	7	6	■ ■	350–550	665–1045
balloon-back dining chair	7	6	■	100–200	190–380
balloon-back armchair	7	6	■ ■	350–750	665–1425
carved mahogany armchair	8	6	■ ■	500–900	950–1710
armchair with buttoned upholstery	7	6	■ ■	400–800	760–1520
mahogany dining chairs with carved rails (set of four)	7	7	■ ■	350–600	665–1140
pair of neo-Gothic hall chairs	7	8	■ ■	150–300	285–570
neo-Gothic X-framed stool	7	8	■ ■ ■	400–800	760–1520
Chests					
mahogany secretaire	8	7	■ ■	350–650	665–1235
oak/walnut Wellington	8	6	■ ■	500–800	950–1520

Qualities on a scale 1-10   ■ Rare   ■ ■ Very rare   ■ ■ ■ Extremely rare

Object	Quality of manufacture	Quality of design and/or decoration	Rarity	Price (£)	Price ($)
Cupboards					
burr walnut double wardrobe	8	7	■ ■	300–600	570–1140
neo-Gothic cupboard	7	6	■ ■ ■	500–1000+	950–1900+
Desks					
mahogany cylinder-top pedestal desk	7	6	■ ■	600–1000+	1140–1900+
walnut roll-top desk	7	7	■	400–800	760–1520
davenport	7	7	■	600–1000+	1140–1900+
'Aesthetic'-style writing desk	7	6	■ ■	400–800	760–1520
Mirrors					
mahogany cheval mirror	7	6	■	200–400	380–760
pair of Italian giltwood girandoles	7	7	■ ■	600–900	1140–1710
Miscellaneous					
mahogany adjustable dumb waiter	7	7	■ ■	400–800	760–1520
coromandel and cut-brass inlaid writing box	8	7	■ ■	300–600	570–1140
mahogany boot jack with turned uprights	7	7	■ ■	100–200	190–380
Screens					
walnut cheval firescreen	8	7	■ ■	400–1000	760–1900
four-leaf scrapwork screen	6	6	■ ■	800–1000+	1520–1900+
pair of pole-screens	8	7	■ ■	700–1000	1330–1900
Settees					
carved walnut chaise longue	7	7	■ ■ ■	500–1000+	950–1900+
double-ended settee	7	6	■ ■ ■	500–900	950–1710
confidante	7	7	■ ■ ■	800–1000+	1520–1900+
reclining day bed	7	6	■ ■	600–800	1140–1520

Qualities on a scale 1-10   ■ Rare   ■ ■ Very rare   ■ ■ ■ Extremely rare

Object	Quality of manufacture	Quality of design and/or decoration	Rarity	Price (£)	Price ($)
Sideboards					
mahogany breakfront	7	7	■	300–600	570–1140
mahogany and inlaid pedestal	8	6	■ ■	750–1000+	1425–1900+
Stands					
mahogany hall-stand	7	6	■ ■	500–700	950–1330
bentwood coat stand	8	8	■ ■	250–500	475–950
carved bear umbrella stand	7	5	■ ■	450–900	855–1710
Stools					
rosewood with 'X'-scroll supports	7	7	■ ■	250–500	475–950
carved mahogany with needlework seat	7	6	■ ■	300–600	570–1140
pair of walnut and inlaid window seats	8	7	■ ■ ■	500–900	950–1710
Tables					
walnut work table	7	6	■ ■	700–900	1330–1710
mahogany library table	7	7	■	500-1000+	950–1900+
inlaid games table	7	6	■ ■	300–600	570–1140
burr walnut centre table	8	7	■ ■	800–1000+	1520–1900+
mahogany and giltwood console table	8	7	■ ■ ■	700–1000	1330–1900
oak dressing table	7	7	■ ■	400–700	760–1330
carved mahogany dressing table	7	7	■ ■ ■	500–800	950–1520
walnut loo table with inlaid decoration	8	7	■ ■	400–600	760–1140
papier-mâché pedestal table with mother-of-pearl inlay	8	6	■ ■ ■	850–1000+	1615–1900+
Whatnots					
burr walnut canterbury/whatnot	7	7	■ ■	300–600	570–1140
five-tier whatnot	7	7	■ ■	350–700	665–1330

Qualities on a scale 1-10   ■ Rare   ■ ■ Very rare   ■ ■ ■ Extremely rare

Object	Quality of manufacture	Quality of design and/or decoration	Rarity	Price (£)	Price ($)
Vitrines					
brass-framed vitrine	7	6	■ ■	500–800	950–1520
Louis XVI-style mahogany and gilt-bronze display cabinet	7	6	■ ■ ■	800–1000+	1520–1900+
walnut specimen table	7	7	■ ■	250–500	475–950
curved oak display cabinet	7	6	■	450–750	855–1425

Qualities on a scale 1-10　　■ Rare　　■ ■ Very rare　　■ ■ ■ Extremely rare

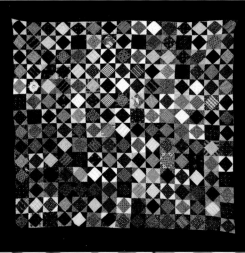

CHAPTER TWO

TEXTILES

Patchwork quilt
Height: 240 cm
Sold: Phillips, London, 1/10/87
Price: £198

The general opinion today is that alone among the applied arts of the nineteenth century, textiles and embroidery remained to a great extent free of excess ornament, over-decoration and distortion. In their day, however, they were often sharply criticized. The medieval revival brought textiles into close association with the Church, and associated them with a tradition which was entirely misconceived. Long before William Morris entered the field with his patterns of pomegranates and roses, dissected and laid flat in formal designs, a great deal of hand-embroidered work was reviled and discredited by contemporary leaders in the field of design.

The trouble was that the Victorians somehow confused medieval embroidery and its themes with those who stitched it. Embroidery, they believed, should embody the qualities that were symbolized in silks and wools, and those who stitched it should be detached in every way from the material world. In their romantic passion for the new age of chivalry, they came to believe that the very act of embroidery was symbolic of chastity and piety. Thus, as early as the 1840s, churchmen in particular voiced their dilemma, finding it 'inexpressibly painful' to see similar or even identical patterns on an altar-cloth and in a drawing room. Gilbert Scott, arch-architect of the neo-

---

Morris & Co. printed cotton
Bird and Anemone
98 × 165 cm
Paul Reeves, London
Price: £160

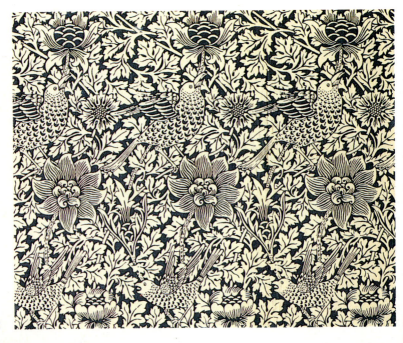

Woolwork cheval firescreen
Height: 112.5 cm
Richard Breeze, London
Price: £390

Woolwork picture
Height: 58.7 cm
Richard Breeze, London
Price: £270

Gothic movement, sarcastically compared the haloes on contemporary church embroidery as 'unhappily suggestive of the metal plates of the Sun Fire Insurance Company'.

CREWEL WORK AND EMBROIDERY

One of the prime movers in the reform of the riotous cottage-garden attitude to flower patterns was Agnes Blencowe, who published twelve working patterns of flowers taken directly from medieval religious tapestries and embroideries, and founded the Ladies Ecclesiological Society to further the proper discipline of religious embroidery. Tudor roses and formal leaves and flowers

replaced the free interpretations of the first few years of Queen Victoria's reign.

Crewel work, essentially a method of adding colour and design to undyed 'sadde' or drab linen, was principally used for bed-hangings and curtains in seventeenth-century bedchambers. The woollen yarns or worsteds used then were mainly blues and greens, the patterns of vines and creepers curling and twining upwards, growing from small green mounds and hills around the bottom border. Beds were richly decked with at least three curtains, each 1.8 m (6 ft) long and 3.2 m (3½ yd) wide, three valances, each 6 m (6½ yd) in length, three base valances and twelve matching cush-

Screen with needlework panels
Height: 94 cm
Sold: Christie's, Orchardleigh Park,
21/9/87
Price: £242

ions for the bed, stools and chairs in the bedchamber. Victorian crewel bed-hangings, on the other hand, were meagre in comparison. The traditional blues and greens were supplemented with deep yellow and rust red, and were lined with blue or green cotton, since Victorian needlewomen could not achieve the virtually stitchless reverse sides of seventeenth-century work. But then, there was an abundance of embroidery wool, and there was little need to use it sparsely.

DESIGNING FOR MACHINES

It is to William Morris that the credit is generally given for revolutionizing the design of upholstery and furnishing fabrics, although many other furniture designers, Seddon and Morant among them, supervised and commissioned their own patterns for upholstered chairs, sofas, settees, stools and curtain material. Ever since the technical achievements of Arkwright, Crompton and Hargreaves in the second half of the eighteenth century, weaving had moved out of the cottage and into the factory, where wool and cotton were woven by machine in enormous quantities for both the home and export trade. The population of Lancashire was a bare 160,000 in 1701, but by 1801 it had risen to 695,000, almost entirely due to the cotton mills. Farther east, Halifax and Leeds were correspondingly prosperous with woven woollen goods, and Bristol in the west and Norwich in the east shipped woollen goods to the New World and the Old.

The firm of Morris, Marshall, Faulkner and Co. was prominent in the production of good patterns and designs, together with yarns and silks dyed to the appropriate colours, from their embroidery workshop. This was started in the late 1860s, and in the 1880s was taken over and run by William Morris's daughter May. It must be said, however, that William Morris never paid too much attention to the special demands of woolwork embroidery, and the bulk of his commercial designs were no more than his patterns for wallpapers and fabrics repeated in ready-made transfers or printed on canvas. All the same, they were a welcome alternative to Berlin woolwork — patterns, printed on squared paper in every women's magazine and journal, for tea cosies, cushion covers, fire screens, blotters, slippers and almost anything that could be made in wool-embroidered canvas.

CHASTITY AND AYRSHIRE WHITEWORK

In keeping with the chaste and modest image of a gentlewoman, her clothes reflected her purity with an increasing quantity of soft muslins and nets, preferably white. No longer expensive and hand-woven, these diaphanous fabrics were being machine made from the beginning of the nineteenth century. Mrs Jameson of Ayrshire was the principal innovator of a new technique of finely embroidered whitework in the traditions of eighteenth-century tambour work, but in which the embroiderer did not need to use a frame.

Introduced in about 1814, 'Ayrshire work' was made by quick-fingered women in their homes, in increasing volume until the mid-1860s, and was used for baby linen, christening robes, wedding veils, skirts and underskirts as well as gentlemen's dress shirts. Printed with transfers of designs, the lengths of cloth were supplied to women under contract who embroidered it with satin stitch and stem stitch, interspersed with cut-out panels filled with needlepoint lace. Thousands of women and children were employed in Scotland, Ireland and the traditional centres of lace-making round Nottingham, Derby and Leicester. In 1857 it was estimated that there were 80,000 embroiderers working from home in Scotland and about 400,000 in Ireland.

It was considered far more humane for these women to work at home, but the hours were longer than factory hours – from six in the morning with two hours off for rest and meals, often until ten at night. Like the women and children employed to knot fine silk carpets in Persia, many

Embroidered ivory silk flounce
Width: 74.8 cm
Sold: Phillips, London, 16/7/87
Price: £143

of them were blind by the time they were twenty. Lace-making was as bad, if not worse. The average wage for making fine Nottingham lace was two shillings and sixpence a week. Children were threading needles and pulling threads from three years old upwards, and by the time they were eight or nine they were doing all the simple work needed in a piece before more skilled, older hands took over and completed it.

Fine whitework embroidery, and Ayrshire work in particular, was dealt a punishing blow in 1861 when the outbreak of the American Civil War and the blockade of ports prevented cargoes of cotton reaching England, and starved the looms of Lancashire. By the time cotton was again available, Swiss machine-em-

broidery had usurped hand-embroidery; it was so cheap that it even undercut the price of hand-embroidered cotton in America as well as Europe. In the early 1870s French machine-embroidered cottons, ironically called 'broderie anglaise' after the Ayrshire whitework it supplanted, killed off the hand-embroidered whitework industry except for rare commissions for traditional christening robes and wedding dresses.

QUILTING – A COMFORTABLE COMMUNITY AFFAIR

Quiltmaking was quite a different matter from whitework. It was a traditional activity which had been handed down from generation to generation and was generally done by groups of women who gossiped as they stitched, making warm bedcovers for their families, or intricate cord-quilting with embroidery for a girl's dowry chest.

The best-known quilts are those made by the wives of miners in Durham and in Wales, and of fishermen in the West Country. However, quilting was by no means confined to the poor and needy. Although classified as 'plain sewing' and therefore not really suitable for stitching in the drawing room or parlour, mothers and maiden aunts, nursery maids and industrious children all made quilts in varying degrees of complexity. Some of the prettiest patchwork quilts were made from scraps of eighteenth-century sprigged chintzes, which were copied in coarser cottons and supplied, ready-cut in octagonal shapes, as 'quilt kits'.

The linings for babies' cots and cribs, as well as their caps, bonnets and often much of their other clo-

Woolwork sliding firescreen
Height: 86.5 cm
Richard Breeze, London
Price: £385

thing, were made in quilted white satin. Children learned the technique by using red thread at first so that the pattern was easily visible, and then, as their dexterity improved, fine white stitching. Professional quilters, often men, were still cord-quilting skirts of wedding dresses in the early nineteenth century, and in America the fashion for hand-stitched quilted skirts continued long after machine-quilted cloth was being produced in the factories of Europe.

America had relatively little wool, either for clothes or for bedcovers,

but it did have a surfeit of cotton, which was quilted to provide a warm material. Quilted bedcovers were made in every home, and 'quilting bees' were an important part of life for isolated homesteaders. Most girls took a dowry of quilts, both patchwork and whitework, with them when they married, often as many as 47

American embroidered quilt
280 × 260 cm
Sold: Phillips, London, 1/10/87
Price: £198

SAMPLERS AND PLAIN SEWING

In contrast to embroidery, hand-stitched samplers flourished in the nineteenth century, although they became much more stereotyped than they had been in previous centuries. Samplers, or 'essemplaires', were to fabrics what pattern books were to cabinet-makers and furniture-makers – examples of patterns and variations which could be supplied by merchants seeking commissions. In the seventeenth and eighteenth centuries they included fine examples of lacework, cutwork, and drawn-thread work as well as embroidery in a variety of stitches.

Stitching samplers had always been a method of teaching children several disciplines at the same time: apart from demonstrating the skill of a young embroiderer through the actual embroidery stitches, they frequently figured alphabets and numbers as well as an improving or moral verse or text. In the eighteenth century, with the founding of more than 1,700 charity schools up and down the English countryside, samplers were an essential part of the curriculum for girls, and sometimes boys as well. But the primary principle behind these compulsory pieces of work was their evidence of a girl's proficiency in needlework when she applied for work to one of the wealthy households, as laundry maid, linen maid, and, eventually, ladies' maid, the highest post in service to which a girl from a charity school could hope to aspire.

In addition to absorbing spelling and counting as well as a multitude of embroidery stitches, samplers were used as a means to teach geography. In the eighteenth century the geography was local, as befitted

twelve. Work began when the engagement was announced, and the last quilt to be made was the white bridal quilt. Many were the superstitions attached to the patterns, the colours and the lucky or unlucky events that took place while the dowry quilts were being made.

the rather small horizons attainable, but as the century wore on, maps of the British Isles became quite a common subject for samplers, with the county boundaries marked out by neat rows of cross-stitch. By the end of the century, as the newspapers became filled with accounts of wars and battles which the British soldiers were fighting, samplers were decorated with maps of Europe. Occasionally a sampler of the entire world can be found, but they are rare.

Visible proof of a girl's accomplishments was also found in the plain-sewing samplers and darning sam-plers, which mainly belong to the nineteenth century. They are not as appealing visually as cross-stitch samplers, which had verses, little animals, birds, foliage and flowers, but as touching little scraps of social history they are fascinating. Some plain-sewing samplers are arranged like little books, with each page de-

---

Needlework sampler
Height: 55.3 cm
Sold: Phillips, London, 12/3/87
Price: £264

voted to a particular garment in miniature: pinafores, underskirts, stockings minutely darned, babies' clothes and petticoats, stitched to flannel pages, each of which is edged with a different type of hem stitch or border stitch.

Plain-sewing samplers entered the curriculum of charity schools at the

Needlework sampler
Height: 61.3 cm
Sold: Phillips, London, 29/5/86
Price: £374

end of the eighteenth century, but do not seem to have been made in any great numbers after the first few decades of the nineteenth century. Because of their humble station in life, few of them have survived intact. Darning samplers, which seem to date from the same period, are a little less rare; they were revived in the early years of the twentieth century and were made in great numbers in schools during the depression years of the twenties, presumably to

reinforce the necessity of 'make do and mend'.

It is unfortunate that artificially dyed yarns came on the market in England during the latter part of the 1860s, because the colours in many of the cross-stitch samplers made after that date have faded and become unattractive, and, no matter how fine the work, these samplers have lost their value to a great extent. A particularly virulent orange was the first successful aniline dye, followed by pinks, mauves, violets, and then blues and greens. Many samplers are made with a mixture of vegetable- and chemical-dyed yarns, which has made them fade patchily and unattractively.

SHAWLS AND WRAPS

It is difficult to pinpoint the precise moment when a shawl became an item of dress in its own right. Many portraits and paintings with figures from the mid-eighteenth century, and occasionally earlier, show women with draperies falling gracefully just below the shoulderline and over their forearms, very much in the manner of a shawl. Many of the ladies in Thomas Gainsborough's portraits wear silk stoles thickly edged with hand-made lace, or finely embroidered muslins.

In that curious cross-pollination of fashion and war, it was while the Napoleonic Wars were at their most ferocious that the Empress Josephine first set the fashion for wearing soft cashmere shawls. The East India Company had certainly been sending shawls to England from India long before; shawls were being made in Norwich, traditional home of fine wool cloth in England, as early as 1775; and in 1785 a shawl-making

Left to right: **Norwich silk shawl,
two woollen turnover shawls**
154 × 154 cm, 138 × 144 cm,
140 × 140 cm
Sold: Phillips, London 9/4/87
Prices: £77, £50 & £61

industry was established in Edinburgh, copying Indian shawls. It was
the beautifully romantic, full-length
portrait of the Empress sitting on a
mossy bank in a forest, painted by
Pierre-Paul Prud'hon in about 1804,
that started the fashion. Wrapped
elegantly about her is an 'Indian red'
shawl, about a sari length long,
banded with a formal pattern and
richly embroidered at either end.

It was not until the early 1820s
that a definite reference occurs to
shawls as an Englishwoman's fashion
accessory. A ladies' magazine of
1827 reports that 'Cachemire
shawls, with a white ground, and a
pattern of coloured flowers or green
foliage, are now much worn in out-
door costumes, especially for the
morning walk; the mornings being
rather chilly [it was September],
these warm envelopes are almost
indispensable. We are sorry, however, to find our modern belles so
tardy in adopting those coverings',
which ought now to succeed to the
light appendages of summer cos-
tume.' The high-waisted, clinging,
filmy dresses of the period, which
many young girls dampened to make

51

them cling to the figure, were hardly suitable for the cool autumn weather.

JACQUARD AND PAISLEY

At about the same time, portraits of wealthy German merchants and aristocratic young girls also feature Indian shawls similar to the Empress Josephine's, though rather more robust and thickly fringed, which was the fashion during the early Biedermeier period. The jacquard loom, invented in Lyons in 1805, did not have a disastrous effect on the production of English hand-loomed shawls until the late 1820s, although it was installed in Vienna as early as 1813. 'Viennese shawls' with Oriental patterns competed with cashmere shawls from India, and were supplied to Germany and Italy. One firm in particular, Burde & Arbather, produced work of such high quality that its shawls won a gold medal in 1833 and 1835 at the Industrial Products Exhibition in Vienna.

Norwich shawl
125 × 125 cm
Sold: Phillips, London, 9/4/87
Price: £110

Printed Paisley shawl
119 × 117 cm
Sold: Phillips, London, 9/4/87
Price: £132

In Britain, jacquard looms were first installed in Edinburgh weaving sheds in the late 1820s, and the industry expanded so fast that its cloths and their patterns became world renowned. The most famous pattern was named after the small town of Paisley, west of Glasgow; it gave its name to an ancient Persian pattern known as the 'boteh' which travelled across Central Asia and into India with the Mughal Emperors, and may originally have represented the eye of a peacock feather. Early 'Paisley' patterns were woven in Edinburgh by the firm of Gibbs and Macdonald; the shawls were one-sided (the reverse was cropped and trimmed) but they were worn folded, corner to corner, with the right side showing. In the late 1840s John Cunningham of Paisley developed a jacquard-woven shawl with a pattern on both sides, and in 1854 John Clabburn of the Norwich shawl-making firm of Clabburn Sons & Crisp, perfected and patented a completely reversible shawl.

Shawls were briefly out of fashion's favour before the arrival of the crinoline at the end of the 1850s. But there was virtually no alternative to a shawl for warmth and outer covering once this fashion took hold, and shawl-making became a profitable and successful industry in Britain until the last decade of the century. Having been persuaded to take to the crinoline by Empress Eugénie of France, the women of Europe abandoned it shortly after the Franco-Prussian War, and the Viennese and French shawl-weaving industries declined. However, expensive woven silk shawls and fabrics such as brocades and damasks remained fashionable for those who could afford them.

Object	Quality of manufacture	Quality of design and/or decoration	Rarity	Price (£)	Price ($)
Costume					
girl's silk dress, piped trim	7	7	■ ■	250–500	475–950
shot-silk gown, piped trim and ruched shoulders	7	7	■ ■	100–200	190–380
two-piece silk gown, brocaded decoration and lace trim	8	7	■ ■	75–150	142–285
alpaca gown with hooped bustle skirt	7	7	■ ■	60–120	114–228
two-piece satin gown, brocaded decoration and bustle skirt	7	7	■ ■ ■	100–200	190–380
glazed cotton petticoat, padded and quilted	7	6	■ ■	40–100	76–190
silk cape	7	7	■ ■	30–60	57–114
lawn cap, piped and ruched trim, frilled edge	7	6	■ ■	25–50	47–95
pair of lady's black kid boots	7	6	■ ■	25–50	47–95
pair of lady's satin shoes	7	6	■ ■	20–60	38–114
pair of lady's worsted shoes, embroidered in silks	7	7	■ ■	120–240	228–456
Crewel work					
coverlet	8	7	■ ■	250–500	475–950
pair of curtains	7	7	■ ■	300–600	570–1140
cushion cover	8	7	■	100–300	190–570
Furnishing fabrics					
pair of printed velvet curtains by Morris & Co.	9	9	■ ■ ■	800–1000	1520–1900
pair of chintz curtains by Morris & Co.	9	9	■ ■ ■	700–900	1330–1710
embroidered ivory silk flounce	7	6	■ ■	100–200	190–380
pair of embroidered ivory silk curtains	7	7	■ ■	300–500	570–950

Qualities on a scale 1-10   ■ Rare   ■ ■ Very rare   ■ ■ ■ Extremely rare

Object	Quality of manufacture	Quality of design and/or decoration	Rarity	Price (£)	Price ($)
Lace					
'Ayrshire whitework' wedding veil	7	6	■ ■	100–200	190–380
broderie-anglaise collar	6	6	■ ■ ■	50–100	95–190
lace collar	8	6	■ ■	75–150	140–285
Brussels lace flounce	8	7	■ ■	500–800	950–1520
Normandy lace bedspread	7	7	■ ■ ■	100–200	190–380
Brussels triangular shawl with appliqué decoration	8	8	■ ■ ■	75–150	142–285
Honiton matching collar and cuffs	7	6	■ ■	40–100	76–190
Honiton bridal veil with appliqué decoration	7	7	■ ■	80–160	152–304
Carrickmacross flounce	7	6	■ ■	30–60	57–114
Carrickmacross collar	7	6	■ ■	25–50	47–95
Needlework					
embroidered picture in silk thread	8	8	■ ■ ■	500–800	950–1520
embroidered three-leaf screen	7	7	■ ■	200–400	380–760
embroidered linen handkerchief	7	7	■ ■	150–350	285–665
sampler (letters and numerals)	7	7	■	100–200	190–380
sampler (letters, numerals, picture/map)	8	7	■ ■	350–700	665–1330
plain-sewing/darning sampler	7	5	■ ■	150–500	285–950
purse embroidered in petit-point silks	8	7	■ ■	75–150	142–285
worsted cover with panel embroidered in gros point	7	6	■ ■	70–140	133–266

Qualities on a scale 1-10   ■ Rare   ■ ■ Very rare   ■ ■ ■ Extremely rare

Object	Quality of manufacture	Quality of design and/or decoration	Rarity	Price (£)	Price ($)
Oriental					
Japanese silk kimono, printed decoration	7	8	■ ■	40–100	76–190
Japanese silk kimono, embroidered decoration	8	8	■ ■	200–400	380–760
Chinese silk coverlet, embroidered decoration	8	8	■ ■	350–750	665–1425
Chinese silk robe, embroidered decoration	8	8	■ ■	100–300	190–570
Chinese silk skirt, embroidered decoration	8	8	■ ■	50–250	95–475
Chinese self-embroidered silk shawl	7	8	■ ■	40–100	76–190
Chinese silk shawl, embroidered decoration	8	8	■ ■	60–150	114–285
Delhi embroidered shawl	7	7	■ ■	40–80	76–152
Kashmir embroidered shawl	8	7	■ ■	150–500	285–950
Quilting					
plain pattern patchwork bedcover	7	7	■ ■	150–300	285–570
printed cotton patchwork bedcover	7	7	■ ■	200–400	380–760
whitework bedcover	8	6	■ ■	150–450	285–855
white satin baby's coat	7	6	■ ■ ■	200–400	380–760

Qualities on a scale 1-10　　　■ Rare　　　■ ■ Very rare　　　■ ■ ■ Extremely rare

Object	Quality of manufacture	Quality of design and/or decoration	Rarity	Price (£)	Price ($)
Shawls					
Indian Paisley pattern	8	8	■ ■	100–200	190–380
Paisley by John Cunningham Ltd.	8	7	■ ■	150–250	285–475
Paisley pattern by Gibbs & Macdonald of Edinburgh	8	7	■ ■	100–200	190–380
Norwich, by Clabburn & Crisp	8	7	■ ■	100–200	190–380
Paisley, silk, printed with 'moon' pattern	8	8	■ ■ ■	200–300	380–570
Paisley, wool, with printed decoration	7	6	■	40–100	76–190
Paisley, wool, with woven decoration	7	6	■ ■	80–200	152–380
Paisley, silk, with printed decoration	6	6	■ ■	50–150	95–285
Norwich, wool and silk, with woven decoration	7	7	■ ■	60–200	114–380
Lyons, silk	8	7	■ ■ •	40–100	76–190
Tapestry					
cushion cover	8	8	■ ■	200–500	380–950
firescreen	8	8	■ ■	300–600	570–1140
Woolwork					
picture	8	7	■ ■	350–800	665–1520
'ship' picture	8	8	■ ■ ■	600–900	1140–1710
firescreen	7	7	■	250–500	475–950
tea cosy	7	7	■ ■	100–300	190–570
cushion cover	8	7	■ ■	250–500	475–950

Qualities on a scale 1-10   ■ Rare   ■ ■ Very rare   ■ ■ ■ Extremely rare

CHAPTER THREE

CERAMICS

Coalport plate commemorating
W.G. Grace's Century of Centuries
Diameter: 28.7 cm
Sold: Phillips, London, 22/10/86
Price: £440

In 1774 Josiah Wedgwood moved from Great Newport Street to open his new showrooms in Greek Street, just off Soho Square. There he displayed his wares, in cabinets along the walls and on immaculately polished tables laid as though a dinner party were about to begin. Salesmen hovered discreetly among the columns which rose from polished floor to plastered ceiling, and on stands against the walls, sets of vases were arranged in patterns and groups which every few days were – in Wedgwood's own words – 'so alter'd, revers'd and transformed as to render the whole a new scene'. His declared aim was 'to amuse and divert, please, astonish – nay even to ravish the Ladies'.

CONTINENTAL PORCELAIN AND ENGLISH BONE CHINA

Until the 1790s, all the fine porcelain of Europe came from France, Austria and Germany, where the great porcelain factories of Sèvres, Dresden, Meissen and Vienna dominated one of the richest of luxury trades. Eighteenth-century British porcelain was soft paste, not the hard paste porcelain made by the great Continental factories, but in 1810 a successful formula was developed for making bone china.

The best-known porcelain factories in early nineteenth-century England and Wales are Coalport, Copeland (late Spode), Derby, Minton, Worcester, and Rockingham. Slightly less well-known are Chamberlain of Worcester, Nantgarw, Pinxton and Madeley. Almost without exception they made soft paste porcelain, as distinct from Continental hard paste porcelain. The styles and designs were imitative

of Sèvres, although the British were not at home with the free, asymmetrical, swirling rococo shapes that were enjoying a rich revival under Napoleon, Josephine and the French Empire.

The Vienna Porcelain Factory's heavily decorated and gilded style became fashionable in Britain in the mid-1850s, partly due to the rich examples shown at the Great Exhibition but mainly because of a shift in political friendships. After the Princess Royal married Frederick of Prussia in 1857, the French and the British withdrew from their close alliance, which had culminated in the armies of both nations fighting side by side in the Crimea only a few years before. The Vienna Porcelain Factory was forced into closure in 1864 by competition from Bohemian porce-

Liverpool creamware commemorative jug
Height; 28.6 cm
Sold: Phillips, London, 10/6/87
Price: £825

**Grainger Lee & Co. bone china
'Japan' pattern tea service**
Height (teapot): 22.7 cm
Sold: Phillips, London, 10/6/87
Price: £990

lain factories in and around Karlsbad, which began to make cheaper wares, and quite openly used the famous Vienna Porcelain Factory mark. Today there is probably more Bohemian porcelain marked with an illicit 'Shield Barry' than there are genuine pieces with authentic marks.

George IV, during the long regency and his brief reign, was a passionate collector of Sèvres porcelain. True, he commissioned a dinner service from the Vienna Porcelain Factory, consisting of more than three hundred pieces most lavishly gilded and painted with flowers, which took several years to make and has been called 'the English service', but in the end he rejected it in favour of a crate of Tokay wine and the service was split up and dispersed.

Undoubtedly, it was King George's passion for Sèvres which caused so many porcelain factories in England to try to compete with the Continental factories, producing heavily gilded services with an increasing range of ground colours. In addition to characteristic 'Bleu de Sèvres', Coalport introduced a deep maroon colour early in the nineteenth century and two distinctive greens – a deep 'Sardinian' green and a pale apple green, also made by Copeland in the 1840s. There was 'Bleu du Roi', 'Rose du Barry' and pale turquoise too, all notably Victorian ground colours, made possible by new pigments, glazes and firing techniques.

It is not easy to follow the nineteenth-century ebb and flow of styles in porcelain, except in terms of the subjects that were chosen as decoration. The French influence of the first two decades or so is evident, in decoration which was based on the fantasy countrysides of Watteau and Fragonard, which typified the beautiful and unreal rococo world of Louis XV and his famous mistress, Madame du Barry. In the hands of the English, this degenerated into images of overblown flower gardens, with the notable exception of 'botanical' decoration, which was extremely fine. At the same time, an aspect of the Romantic Movement manifested itself in porcelain painted with landscapes with dramatic Gothic ruins.

In small, decorative cabinet wares there was a revival of eighteenth-century flower-encrusted designs, previously made in soft-paste porcelain in Bow, Chelsea and Derby. Every leading maker of bone china made bouquets and bocages, pot pourri vases and little baskets and dishes covered with tiny flowers and leaves. The Derby factory brought out their old moulds to make a new series of figures and mantelpiece ornaments, which they produced from the 1860s onwards; these were recognizably Victorian in their colouring and lack of crisp detail. In 1876 the Derby Crown Porcelain Company, an entirely new and unrelated factory, also began to make fine bone china tableware.

PARIAN AND MOULDED STONEWARE

Advanced techniques of manufacture now gave the porcelain factories an entirely new clay 'body', Parian, which was developed to rival the famous eighteenth-century Derby 'biscuit' and allowed them to make bone china. Parian is a substance which has a relatively large kaolin content, but strictly speaking is not a

Samson porcelain figures from the Commedia dell'Arte
Height: 35.5 cm
Sold: Phillips, London, 10/6/87
Price £715

true porcelain. It was developed by Copeland & Garrett in 1842, though several other porcelain factories were experimenting with similar formulae and Minton produced a slightly different version only two years later. The intention behind its development was to produce a substitute for marble, to meet the growing demand for classical heads, busts and figures. It was Herbert Minton who gave Parian its name, derived from a particular variety of marble found on the Greek island of Paros.

By using a pantograph (a method of reducing a model in size), groups and figures could be reduced precisely to scale and be made suitable for use in the home. Among the first classical figures to be so diminished in stature was the Venus de Milo, soon followed by many others; such was the paradoxical attitude of the Victorians to modesty and morality that several dozen, different nude figures in many different sizes were exhibited at the Crystal Palace and sold to an eager public. 'Statuary' Parian, as this blond simulated marble is called, was shortly followed by another variety, 'domestic' Parian, which was heat-resistant and suitable for making moulded jugs, teapots and other similar ware. Some of the most ornate and ambitious moulded Parianware was made in America by the United States Pottery, Vermont, between 1847 and 1858. Many designs were based on their English counterparts, with flowers, leaves and vine motifs, but particularly American were the jugs, pitchers and vases based on ears of maize (corn).

The great popularity of relief-moulded wares encouraged the makers of stoneware to produce a similar range of jugs, pitchers and

vases on both sides of the Atlantic, many of them very similar to Parian-ware designs – some actually made in the same moulds. This has naturally resulted in some confusion between the two. Moulded Parian-ware is essentially matt and un-

Portobello cow creamer
Height: 11.2 cm
Sold: Phillips, London, 10/6/87
Price: £484

glazed, a factor which told against it with the Victorian housewife, who found it difficult to keep clean. Moulded stoneware, however, has a shiny surface and is altogether more amenable to soap and water. Plain moulded whiteware was also produced in America, again frequently based on English patterns, and difficult to distinguish from English whiteware unless it is marked with an American factory mark.

BELLEEK

The Belleek factory of Fermanagh in Ireland produced an extremely distinctive line of highly decorative 63

Belleek 'Neptune' pattern tea service
Height (teapot): 24.3 cm
Sold: Christie's Scotland, 30/10/87
Price: £495

cabinet ware, patented in 1858, and glazed with a curious mother-of-pearl glaze. This ware was called Belleek. The work was so fine that it was used by jewellers for flower-heads, particularly sprays of lilies-of-the-valley. It might almost be said that this factory's ware was closer to true rococo than any other in Britain — its range of shells, coral, sea horses and marine life is quite remarkable.

AMERICAN DEVELOPMENTS

American attempts to establish porcelain factories had begun in the late eighteenth century but were unsuccessful and shortlived. William Ellis Tucker of Philadelphia set up in business in 1826, decorating 'blanks' imported from France, and later produced a range of porcelain under the name of the American Porcelain Company. The wares are almost indistinguishable from earlier French imports to the United States, and in 1838 the company closed, unable to compete with the far cheaper wares from Europe.

The widespread disruption by the Civil War meant that little or no industrial advances were made in America until the 1870s. Most of the major porcelain factories established after that date were centred around Trenton, New Jersey, and East Liverpool, Ohio, but the main impetus for American porcelain began with the Union Porcelain Works at Greenpoint, New York. Here Karl Muller, a German brought in by the owners Thomas C. Smith and his brother, initiated the production of European hard paste porcelain in 1874, resulting in such historic pieces as the

Century Vase and the *Liberty Cup*.

In 1887 Knowles, Taylor and Knowles, an American porcelain factory in East Liverpool, Ohio, brought Joshua Poole over from Belleek and the factory made similar, pearly, semi-translucent wares until fire destroyed the entire works in 1889. Rebuilt, the company began to make its own versions of Belleek which it called 'Lotus' ware; it also had considerable success in producing *pâte-sur-pâte*. This technique was developed by Marc Louis Solon at Sèvres, though it originated in China. Layers of white liquid slip are applied to a coloured ground. They are then pared and carved away so that the final decoration is diaphanous and insubstantial, wreathing the dark-bodied ground with dramatic effect. The delicate ranges made by Knowles, Taylor and Knowles were, however, a minute fraction of the factory's production; by the end of the century it was producing crockery and tableware for hotels on a gigantic scale. The extent of its production can be gauged by the huge size of its factories and plant, which in 1890 covered four hectares (ten acres) of land.

THE DEBT TO WEDGWOOD

English manufacturers had observed that domestic Parian was not unlike Wedgwood's Jasper ware of the 1770s, and pressed plaques stained a more vivid blue than those of Wedgwood and his contemporaries were made up until about 1880. The main producers were the Mayers of Dale Hall, descendants of the Staffordshire potter Elijah Mayer, maker of black basaltes and bamboo ware and a contemporary of the great Josiah Wedgwood.

Wedgwood was never greatly concerned with the development of porcelain – what was the need? Continental factories made the best European porcelain and there was a massive trade with China in its fine porcelains. What did concern him

Elton vase
Height: 51 cm
Sold: Phillips, London, 24/3/87
Price: £242

was that Britain needed tableware of a reasonable quality, standard, durability and quantity, and at a reasonable price, which he strove to supply. Following his lead, the potteries of the United Kingdom developed a unique range of fine stonewares and, unlike the rest of Europe, produced a wide variety of tableware specifically for the middle market, which could not afford expensive, imported porcelain or British bone china. The stoneware was made from a refined clay body mixed with a variety of vitreous frit which rendered it smooth, white, durable and heat-resistant. The origins of the entire family of ironstones, stone chinas and American whiteware go back to Wedgwood's ceaseless search for a suitable material for everyday domestic tableware, which culminated in his fine-bodied creamware in 1774.

It was not only in the domestic market that there was a gap – there were also great opportunities for exporting domestic wares to Britain's growing colonies overseas. Eventually, as a result of Wedgwood's experiments, by the 1820s the potteries of Staffordshire, Scotland,

Wales and Worcester had perfected the manufacture of bone china, which filled the holds of merchant ships and the shelves of homes around the world – at least until the colonies became manufacturing nations and began to produce their own.

ETRUSCAN WARE AND TERRACOTTA

The legacy that Josiah Wedgwood left when he died in 1795 was to become the basic repertoire of china manufacture of the nineteenth century. Ornamental Etruscan ware vases and urns in black basaltes with iron red encaustic decoration; fine Jasper ware in 'Wedgwood' blue, sage green, lilac, lavender and black, decorated in white relief with classical scenes, cameo heads, swags and medallions; a breathtaking range of simulated

---

William de Morgan tiles decorated in copper lustre
Height: 17.3 cm
Sold; Phillips, London, 18/6/87
Price: £715

marble and striated stone; polished red stoneware, bambooware and caneware – all these were copied and elaborated upon by every nineteenth-century manufacturer. The debt was publicly acknowledged at the Great Exhibition, where copies of 'Etruscan ware' were much in evidence, though made in terracotta rather than black basaltes, and decorated with classical friezes, figures and scenes.

The first imitator of 'Etruscan ware' seems to have been a small firm at Lowesby in Leicestershire, which made high-quality terracotta as well as more ornamental ware decorated with enamels and gilding, for a brief period from 1835 to 1840. But F. & R. Pratt of Fenton was far better known – a pair of its terracotta vases 1.5 m (5 ft) high was awarded a silver medal by the Society of Arts in 1848. This firm used many illustrations by John Flaxman of Homer's *Iliad* as a basis for its designs. Far more commercial was the range produced by M. H. Blanchard, Son & Co. of Westminster Road, London who, from the 1840s onwards produced terracotta of a uniform standard and colour, a great deal of it decorated by Thomas Battam. Slightly later and more adventurous is the range from W. & T. Wills of Euston Road, London, who produced a deep-red terracotta, hand-carved all over with dragons and Oriental designs in similar fashion to the heavily decorated, imported, Chinese and Japanese ware in the latter part of the century.

MAJOLICA AND FAIENCE

More popular and far more colourful than terracotta was Minton's majolica. It was developed from a body similar to Wedgwood's fine cane-

William de Morgan lustre tile
Height: 21.6 cm
Richard Dennis, London
Price: £200

ware, but in appearance and decoration was often more similar to early tin-glazed Delft and its antecedent, Italian maiolica, apart from the colours; unfortunately, the colour palette of the 1850s included some new chemical pigments, many of which were strident. The colours aside, in domestic items such as game dishes, chestnut dishes, tureens and basket-weave serving dishes, the detail of the modelling is crisp and sharp and the designs are extremely pleasing. Minton's flower-encrusted ware, too, has remarkably fine detail, but, as with so much Victorian decorative art, once the size is increased the harmony of design becomes discordant and the detail is lost.

From the 1870s, when some of the best majolica was being made by Minton and several other factories, fashionable interiors were also decorated with faience. Some of the finest   67

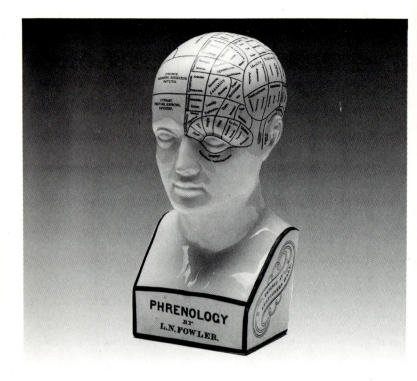

Staffordshire phrenology bust
Height: 37.5 cm
Sold: Bearne's, Torquay, 26/2/87
Price: £418

and most original of the nineteenth-century versions of faience were produced by the Gateshead Art Pottery, a small offshoot of the great Gateshead Glassworks. The designs are impeccable, echoing precisely William Morris's formal, two-dimensional flower patterns, and the pieces were mostly limited to chargers, or large decorative plates. Curiously, these were made from fireclay, a lowly material normally used for making firebricks and tiles.

STAFFORDSHIRE BLUE AND WHITE

It was from the kilns of Staffordshire that the three types of ceramic that epitomize Victoriana came. These were blue-and-white transfer-printed tableware; small pottery figures and groups called 'flatbacks'; and Mason's Patent Ironstone China.

The blue-and-white willow pattern is universally famous; in all its variations it was made by dozens of Staffordshire potteries in stoneware of one kind or another. Willow pattern was so popular that, at the end of the eighteenth century, Enoch Wood of Burslem saw the vast potential market available to him across the Atlantic and became the first manufacturer of blue-and-white tableware made specifically for the American market. It is regrettable to record that in the nineteenth century many of the Staffordshire potteries crated up their factory rejects and sent them overseas. Today these pieces are known as 'flow blue' because the blue pigment failed to remain stable and 'flew' into the glaze or the once-fired biscuit; flow blue is characterized by a considerable amount of blurring in the pattern.

STAFFORDSHIRE FLATBACKS

The figures and groups known as Staffordshire flatbacks were by no means intended for the mass market when they were first produced at the end of the eighteenth century. Many of them were copied from bocage and arbour groups made by Chelsea, Bow and Derby, and, though crude, were bought enthusiastically by rich industrialists and entrepreneurs who had made their fortunes after the demise of the eighteenth-century porcelain factories. These early examples, dating from the 1780s onwards, are quite distinct in colour, glaze and modelling from the later 'flatbacks', which were made in light-coloured clays pressed into moulds which were used repeatedly, and decorated with a distinctly Victorian colour palette – rich dark blue, salmon pink, orange, dark green, acid green, strident flesh pink and black, with a lavish use of old-fashioned oil gilding. Their bold, bright colours and slightly irreverent treatment of important political figures, naval and military leaders and heads of state give the lie to the popular myth that Victorian taste was dull, morbid and lacking in spontaneity.

Willow-pattern meat plate
Length: 43.7 cm
Richard Breeze, London
Price (damaged): £10

MASON'S IRONSTONE

The two sons of Miles Mason – George and Charles – lived to see their Patent Ironstone China become a runaway success from the moment they first took out the patent, in 1813. But it is still surprising that today this brightly coloured, hard earthenware – made by adding ironstone slag to the other constituents of porcelain – should command such high prices. Mason's patterns, often in rich, bright colours, were mass-produced, transfer-printed versions of the expensive, handmade wares that were produced at Worcester in porcelain.

Because of over-expansion and disagreement between the two brothers, the firm of Mason's went bankrupt in 1848, but it was shrewdly bought by Frances Morley, together with all the moulds and patterns, just after the Great Exhibition. From 1862 the company became Geo. Ashworth & Brothers, and in

69

order to cut costs and compete with its imitators, production was speeded up, with a resulting decline in quality.

GAUDY WELSH

In Staffordshire, Newcastle, Sunderland and Wales, between about 1820 and 1860, there was a strong rival to Mason's Patent Ironstone, which is less well-known in Britain than it is in America. The generic name is Gaudy Welsh, and it is true that

quantities of this brightly decorated ware were made in the small potteries of Wales. It was exported in all its varieties to America, mostly in cargoes destined for Philadelphia. Cheap, bright and hardwearing jugs,

---

Staffordshire money-box
Height: 17.1 cm
Sold: Christie's, South Kensington,
London, 2/9/85
Price: £495

tea services and bowls were sold by travelling merchants to the growing immigrant populations of Pennsylvania, Illinois, the poorer districts of New York, and Ohio.

Gaudy Welsh is characterized by the use of copper lustre instead of the richer gilding of Mason's patterns. But its designs are not restricted to heavy-quality ironstones, and are found on every variety of body from opaque stonewares to fine, almost translucent, bone china. Export ceased with the outbreak of the American Civil War and its attendant port blockades, but in more recent times reproductions of Gaudy Welsh have been made by many potteries, notably Charles Allerton and Sons of Longton.

AMERICAN WHITEWARE

Although the American potteries were not producing anything which

'Gaudy Welsh' teapot
Height: 12.5 cm
Richard Breeze, London
Price: £20

remotely resembled Staffordshire blue-and-white or Gaudy Welsh, they did manufacture whiteware, made from ironstone, stone china and graniteware. Generally restricted to moulded jugs, pitchers and domestic items, it was produced by the potteries of Trenton, New Jersey and East Liverpool, Ohio, until the last two decades of the nineteenth century, when production of whiteware decorated by printing, and commemorative domestic whiteware, began on an enormous scale, unknown in Britain.

Hand-painted whiteware was produced on a smaller scale in the pottery districts and in Pennsylvania, including a particularly attractive and popular pattern on ironstone known as the 'Lustre Band and Spring'. Like Mason's Patent Ironstone, the design was frequently transfer-printed in order to maintain uniformity, and like Gaudy Welsh it made good use of copper lustre. This attractive ware was made in England and exported to America as well, where it is known by the comfortable name of 'tea leaf' pattern.

Mason's Ironstone dinner plate
Diameter: 27.6 cm
Richard Breeze, London
Price: £40

71

Object	Quality of manufacture	Quality of design and/or decoration	Rarity	Price (£)	Price ($)
Bone china					
Copeland hand-painted and gilt plate	8	6	■ ■	50–100	95–190
Grainger & Lee 'Japan' pattern tea service	7	7	■ ■ ■	800–1000+	1520–1900+
Mason's Ironstone dinner plate	7	6	■	30–80	55–150
Wedgwood black basalt teapot	8	7	■ ■	200–400	380–760
tureen and cover	7	6	■ ■	300–500	570–950
jardinière	7	6	■	100–300	190–570
Wedgwood jasperware Portland vase	8	8	■ ■	500–750	950–1425
Wedgwood black basalt bust	8	7	■ ■	300–450	570–855
harlequin set of twelve Mason's Ironstone jugs	7	6	■ ■	800–1000	1520–1900
Ashworth Bros. Ironstone part dinner service (49 pieces)	7	6	■ ■	700–1000+	1330–1900+
Mason's Ironstone baluster vase	7	6	■ ■	300–500	570–950
Commemorative					
W. G. Grace plate by Coalport	7	7	■ ■	300–500	570–950
Liverpool creamware jug	8	7	■ ■ ■	500–1000	950–1900
Staffordshire plate for Queen Victoria's coronation	6	6	■ ■	200–300	380–570
jug for wedding of Edward, Prince of Wales, and Princess Alexandra	6	6	■ ■	100–200	190–380
Staffordshire mug for wedding of Victoria and Albert	7	6	■ ■	200–400	380–760
Doulton jug for Queen Victoria's Diamond Jubilee	7	7	■	80–150	150–285
jug for Manchester and Liverpool Railway	7	7	■ ■	200–400	380–760
copper lustre jug for Queen Victoria's coronation	7	6	■	100–200	190–380

Qualities on a scale 1-10   ■ Rare   ■ ■ Very rare   ■ ■ ■ Extremely rare

Object	Quality of manufacture	Quality of design and/or decoration	Rarity	Price (£)	Price ($)
Majolica					
teapot modelled as a monkey and a serpent by Minton's	7	7	■ ■	400–600	760–1140
Minton 'Palissy' wall plaque	8	7	■ ■ ■	600–800	1140–1520
tureen and cover modelled as a game pie by Minton's	8	6	■ ■	500–700	950–1330
centrepiece modelled as shells and seaweed by Minton's	8	6	■ ■	400–600	760–1140
George Jones sweetmeat dish	7	7	■ ■ ■	700–900	1330–1710
George Jones jardinière	7	7	■ ■ ■	600–1000+	1140–1900+
Wedgwood jardinière	7	6	■ ■	300–500	570–950
model of a stork incorporating a spill vase	7	5	■ ■	150–300	285–570
fish-paste dish with cover and stand	7	6	■ ■	200–400	380–760
George Jones Stilton cheese dish and cover	7	7	■ ■	250–500	475–950
pair of Minton sweetmeat dishes in the form of figures	8	6	■ ■	300–600	570–1140

Qualities on a scale 1-10   ■ Rare   ■ ■ Very rare   ■ ■ ■ Extremely rare   73

Object	Quality of manufacture	Quality of design and/or decoration	Rarity	Price (£)	Price ($)
Porcelain					
Belleek 'Neptune' tea service (three pieces)	8	6	■ ■	400–600	760–1140
Coalport dessert service (22 pieces)	7	6	■ ■	400–700	760–1330
Crown Derby dessert dish, painted decoration	7	7	■ ■	200–500	380–950
Worcester scent bottle	8	7	■ ■	100–200	190–380
Parian centrepiece by Copeland's	7	7	■ ■	300–500	570–950
pair of Parian busts of Victoria and Albert by Kerr's of Worcester	8	7	■ ■ ■	400–600	760–1140
Parian figure by Minton's	8	7	■ ■	150–750	285–1425
Parian jug	7	6	■	40–120	75–230
Parian bust of Shakespeare by Wedgwood	8	7	■ ■ ■	200–300	380–570
Samson figure	8	7	■ ■	300–1000+	570–1900+
'Lotus' pattern jug by Knowles, Taylor & Knowles	8	. 6	■ ■ ■	450–750	855–1425
set of 12 Worcester plates decorated with game birds	8	6	■ ■	600–900	1140–1710
Minton pâte-sur-pâte two-handled pilgrim vase	8	7	■ ■	400–800	760–1520
pâte-sur-pâte vase by George Jones	7	6	■ ■	300–600	570–1140
Belleek pink ground vase and cover	8	6	■ ■ ■	600–900	1140–1710
Portobello					
cow creamer	7	7	■ ■	300–700	570–1330
figure	7	7	■ ■	200–500	380–950

Qualities on a scale 1-10   ■ Rare   ■ ■ Very rare   ■ ■ ■ Extremely rare

Object	Quality of manufacture	Quality of design and/or decoration	Rarity	Price (£)	Price ($)
Relief-moulded jugs					
'Pan' by William Ridgway & Co.	7	6	■ ■	75–150	140–285
'Silenus' by Minton's	8	7	■ ■	60–120	115–230
'Harvest Wreath' by Minton's	7	7	■ ■ ■	100–300	190–570
'Bulrush' by Ridgway & Abington	7	7	■ ■	40–60	75–115
'Gothic Ivy' by Brownfield's	7	6	■ ■	50–75	95–140
'Falstaff' by Thomas Furnival & Co.	7	6	■ ■ ■	100–150	190–285
'Garibaldi' by Henry Baggeley	7	6	■ ■ ■	200–400	380–760
'Nineveh' by Ridgway & Abington	7	8	■ ■	75–150	142–285
'Home and Abroad' (Crimean War) by James Pankhurst & Co.	7	5	■ ■ ■	100–200	190–380
'Prince Consort' by Old Hall Earthenware Co. Ltd.	7	7	■ ■ ■	200–500	380–950
'York Minster' by Charles Meigh	7	7	■ ■	75–150	142–285
Staffordshire					
moneybox modelled as a chapel	7	7	■ ■ ■	300–600	570–1140
phrenology bust	6	6	■	250–500	475–950
blue and white willow-pattern tureen and cover	7	7	■	200–400	380–760
portrait figure of cricketer George Parr	6	7	■ ■ ■	500–750	950–1425
portrait figure of Sir George Brown (Crimean War)	7	7	■ ■	100–200	190–380
'Soldier's Return' figure group	7	7	■ ■	150–250	285–475
pair of horse and jockey groups	6	7	■ ■ ■	400–600	760–1140
figure of 'Jumbo' the elephant	6	7	■ ■	75–150	140–285
lion and lamb group	7	7	■ ■	250–500	475–950
pair of greyhounds	7	7	■	100–200	190–380
model of a Dalmatian dog	7	7	■ ■	80–120	150–230
Goss model of 'The Priest's House, Prestbury, Cheshire'	7	5	■ ■	200–300	380–570
Goss model of the 'Abbot's Kitchen, Glastonbury'	7	5	■ ■	150–250	285–475

Qualities on a scale 1-10　　■ Rare　　■ ■ Very rare　　■ ■ ■ Extremely rare

CHAPTER FOUR

METALWORK

Silvered metal figures
Height: 13.8 cm
Sold: Phillips, London, 14/4/87
Price: £528

There were many who predicted gloomily that machines spelt the death of creative art, but many more saw the possibilities they created for producing art for the masses. The blast-furnaces roared, the iron and steel industries grew mightily, and in the end it was the machines them-

selves that caused the revolution which had begun the previous century.

Metal lay at the heart of the Industrial Revolution and it was through its development for technical and mechanical purposes that it entered the ranks of mass-produced ornament at the beginning of Queen Victoria's reign.

Bronze candelabra by E. T. Hurley
Height: 32.5 cm
Michael Carey Inc., New York
Price: $1250

SILVER PLATE, FUSED PLATE AND ELECTROPLATE

By the end of the eighteenth century there were already machines for stamping out hollow ware in copper,

Sheffield plate wine wagon
Length: 41 cm
Sold: Christie's Scotland, 11/11/87
Price: £715

brass and silver, for producing border decoration ready-stamped and decorated, as well as spouts, feet and finials. There were lathes for turning and spinning metals, and mills and rolling machines for mass-producing wrought-iron bars and ingots, sheet metal and tinplate. Where once silver plate had been painstakingly embossed, engraved and chased by hand, all these processes could now be achieved by machines which stamped and raised patterns on thin sheet silver, turning out tea services and dining-table regalia at prices which the wealthy Victorian middle classes could quite easily afford.

For those who could not afford silver plate, fused plate, or 'Sheffield plate' (a name it was given when production moved from the craftsmen of Birmingham to the manufacturers of Sheffield), was readily available, although not for long. It was a simple matter for rolling mills to take over the laborious process of beating out the copper core and the thin silver sheets that were fused to it on both sides. Even so, assembling a fused plate candlestick was more labour-intensive and more time-consuming than stamping out an identical pattern in thin sheet silver and 'loading' or filling it with pitch. The intricate methods of concealing the edges, where the copper core showed, the complicated construction which many fused plate pieces required, no longer made it a cheaper substitute for sterling silver.

In the 1840s electroplating was first used to coat base metals with a layer of pure silver, simply by suspending a suitable base metal in a solution of metallic salts and passing a direct electric charge through it. The results were even more brilliant than fused plate, which was made with sterling silver alloy containing a small proportion of copper. Rolled gold was made using similar methods to fused plate, and electrogilding made it possible to add quasi-ormolu and gilt metal to the list of goods which, without exception, demonstrated their owner's opulence.

At the Great Exhibition, the glittering examples of electroplate exhibited by Elkington's, who had patented the process in 1840, dazzled the visitors. For a while the process was reserved for *objets d'art*, but the inevitable temptation of the fortune to be made by using it for everyday domestic 'silver' was too strong. The fine, restrained lines of fused plate vanished, killed by a process which could coat the most elaborate and tasteless designs with silver in a tenth of the time at a tenth of the cost.

Every style was copied, sometimes more than one at a time, on table silver and tea services. While true goldsmiths and silversmiths produced a dazzling range of heavy, immaculate patterns, the manufacturers of wholesale silver tended to overload their lightweight wares with machine-stamped embossing, die-stamped decorative borders and lead-filled finials, to disguise their flimsiness. Almost without exception, up to the 1870s better designs were made in fused plate, where the process of manufacture dictated a certain simplicity of design.

From the 1870s onwards, how-

Silver-mounted Doulton preserve jar
Height: 11 cm
Sold: Christie's, South Kensington, London, 5/5/87
Price: £154

Christening mug by J. & J. Angell
Height: 10.3 cm
Sold: Christie's, South Kensington, London, 5/5/87
Price: £165

ever, with the strong revival of the 'Queen Anne' style in domestic articles and interior decoration, the silversmiths of Sheffield and the luxury stores of Regent Street settled into a new tradition which has lasted until the present day. The revival of this style led to a revival of other eighteenth-century styles: Corinthian column candlesticks from the Adam period, sauce boats, entrée dishes, sauce and soup tureens modified only slightly from the designs of the latter decades of the eighteenth century remain the standard stock in trade of smiths working in both sterling silver and fused plate. Even so, huge quantities of cheaply made electroplate and fused plate were made from the 1840s onwards, but for the 'silver service' restaurants of the hotel and catering trade. Their simple, functional forms are reminiscent of the Queen Anne style but the quality of materials and finish is on the whole extremely low.

SILVER ABROAD

In France, and on the Continent as a whole, a cheaper version of fused plate was widely made, using a spinning technique which frequently resulted in silverware with a distinctly pink colour, caused by the copper core showing through an extremely thin coating of silver.

Across the Atlantic, American trade with China and Japan resulted in an influx of silver of a lower pure metal content than British sterling silver. These wares were made by Oriental silversmiths to traditional silver patterns.

Some of the best American silver plate was produced after the Civil War, in Philadelphia. The styles were reminiscent of European Empire and

Regency in which classical and neo-classical designs predominated. There were also quantities of *japonaiserie*, and tea services in particular designed in a distinctly Chinese-inspired style.

No form of control or assay was imposed on American silversmiths until after 1860, when the 'sterling' standard was introduced, and the standard of American silver plate varies considerably from state to state. From about 1850 onwards American silver may be stamped 'D', 'C', 'Coin' or 'Pure Coin' to indicate the standard used. American coin silver was alloyed with copper to the ratio of 9:1, whereas in England hallmarked sterling silver is 9.25 pure metal to .75 copper alloy.

Pair of silver salt cellars as Dickensian characters
Height: 13.5 cm
Sold: Christie's Scotland, 28/4/87
Price: £528

KITCHENWARE

In the eighteenth century, most kitchens on the Continent were equipped with a *batterie de cuisine* consisting of a graduated series of hand-beaten copper pots and pans with brass or iron handles. Among these pans were saucepans which, as their name implies, were used over a relatively low heat for making sauces – cooking processes on the Continent had evolved from Roman and Arabic methods and made use of charcoal braziers and raised brick-built hearths, which did not produce a fierce heat. In England and Colonial America, however, cooking was done over an open fire, in heavy-duty cast-iron pots and cauldrons which could withstand great heat.

After the French Revolution, which began in 1789, fugitive chefs from the courts and kitchens of France – Escoffier, Carême, Franatelli and Alexis Soyer among others – fled across the Channel and the vaster seas of the Atlantic, to find dismayingly primitive conditions and equipment which they at once set about improving. In England the familiar array of gleaming copper saucepans,

Copper saucepans
Height (front); 18 cm
Richard Breeze, London
Price: £70 (with lid), £40

stewpans, jelly and mousse moulds, fish and turbot kettles reflects this French influence and dates mainly from the early nineteenth century.

In 1795, a naturalized American and expert in the science of conduction and convection, by the name of Benjamin Thompson of Salem, Mass., arrived in London. During his work and travels in Europe he had been made a Count of the Holy Roman Empire in 1791 by the Elector of Bavaria, and proudly preferred to be known as Count Rumford. Greatly helped by his expertise, cast iron manufacturers began making enclosed cooking ranges, or kitcheners, and it became a practical proposition thenceforward to cook with tin-lined, copper utensils.

America had to work as best it could with heavy cast-iron cooking pots, imported from England or made in their own small iron foundries, until after the upheavals of the Civil War. Thereafter, characteristically, production of kitchenware and gadgets in America went straight from primitive cast iron to sophisticated mass-produced utensils in brightly coloured enamel or aluminium (which was being tried out commercially in America from as early as 1844).

In the second half of the nineteenth century, labour-saving gadgets of all kinds began to proliferate, at first in cast iron and then in cast aluminium alloy, as well as in tinplate. The Chicago World Fair in 1893 proved beyond question that American manufacturers had not only caught up with products from the Old World but had easily outstripped them. But old-fashioned, 'black' hollow ware in cast iron, greatly improved by steam-driven lathe-turning, continued to be made in the traditional factories of

Copper kettle
Height: 25.5 cm
Richard Breeze, London
Price: £70

south Staffordshire for poor homes in Britain and, in vast quantities, for the colonies of the British Empire, until well into this century.

BRASS – FUNCTIONAL AND DECORATIVE

Up to the second half of the eighteenth century, brass had been a difficult and truculent metal to work. But with the greatly increased heat of coke-fired furnaces and the method developed and patented in 1781 for making uniform sheet and ingot in an alloy of uniform proportions, the brass-manufacturing industry expanded swiftly from its traditional centres of Birmingham, Cheadle, Bristol and Wales. By the beginning of the nineteenth century, sheet brass could be rolled, stamped and embossed entirely by machine. Cast brass articles could be reproduced by the hundred, and by the middle of   83

the century, methods of 'sleeving' (coating iron with a thin layer of brass) heralded the arrival of brass bedsteads; these were cheap to make and more hygienic than the old wooden tester or half-tester. Beds were made with bases of drawn steel mesh and, by the end of the nineteenth century, there were mattresses with coiled springs.

Since the labour involved was the same, it was as cheap to cast a highly ornamental article as a plain and simple one, and to reproduce all the earlier patterns for candlesticks, fire tools, fenders, wall brackets, and brass mounts for mantel ornaments, as well as a new range of things never made in brass before. During the 1870s in particular, the market in Britain and America was flooded with excellent reproductions of 'Queen Anne' and 'Adam' brass, turned and finished on machine-pow-

> **Cast bronze Renaissance-style ewers**
> Height: 61.7 cm
> Sold: Christie's, Great Tew Park,
> 28/5/87
> Price: £220

ered lathes, which admirably suited the prevailing trends in decoration of the period.

ORMOLU

In France, ormolu had always been prized and made scrupulously by craftsmen protected by an elaborate system of guilds, such as the *doreurs* and *ciseleurs* who used specific variations of bronze or brass alloy as a base for their gilding. England had never set much store by this type of cast ornament. This was partly because ormolu could be imported freely from France, and partly because the English brass industry lagged so far behind the Continental craftsmen that very little had been made until the end of the eighteenth century. Matthew Boulton's Birmingham factory was one of the few to make ormolu, mainly as elaborate mounts for marble, Blue John urns and classical garnitures. But even then it was more often catalogued as 'gilt brass' than as 'ormolu', and reserved for expensive commissions. In the nineteenth century, however, dozens of English brass foundries took casts indiscriminately from French work and reproduced heavy furniture mounts for early Victorian versions of 'French Empire' and 'rococo' styles. They also manufactured wall brackets in gilt brass, often crudely finished and not of the high quality of French ormolu.

PEWTER AND THE TUDOR REVIVAL

The Medieval and Romantic revival in Britain brought with it a surge in popularity for 'genuine old pewter'. There emerged a big demand for chargers, flagons, tankards, corn and grain measures, and ale, wine and spirit measures. Pewter is essentially an English alloy, and was first made in Roman times using Cornish tin and lead from the Mendip hills. It is an easy alloy to make, requiring no great skill, and was soon made all over Europe in traditional, functional styles which changed very little.

Victorian Romantic revival pewter is generally taken from Tudor forms. Helmets, visors, and the panoply of jousting were all boosted as essential decoration for richly 'Tudorbethan' entrance halls by the Eglinton Tour-

> **Pair of cast brass doorstops**
> Height: 38.2 cm
> Richard Breeze, London
> Price: £90

Pair of brass candlesticks
Height: 31.7 cm
Richard Breeze, London
Price: £80

vessels once they had been checked by the appropriate authorities. In 1878 a uniform 'V.R.' replaced these earlier marks, although the District, Borough or Council code number was retained.

Pewter and its close relation, Britannia Metal, which is a lead-free alloy of tin, copper and antimony, were both used by manufacturers of decorative domestic metals during the nineteenth century. Pewter was given an artificially 'hammered' finish and used for everything from biscuit barrels to clock faces; it was used with remarkable effect for Liberty's Art Nouveau 'Tudric' range. Britannia Metal was often used as a base for electroplating after the 1860s. In its oxidized and tarnished state, with its thin coating of silver long vanished, it can be found on almost every antique market stall in Europe. Anyone with a good eye for silver shapes can pick up a fine teapot or cream jug and will find polishing it an extremely rewarding task.

IRON – THE GREAT REVOLUTION

By the beginning of the nineteenth century, new ironworking methods enabled iron objects to be cast not as they had been, one at a time in handmade moulds, but in sections by the hundred, each one identical. One of the earliest uses for this new mass-production technique was the manufacture of 'Rustick' and 'Gothick' garden furniture. This was still a

Cast-iron umbrella stand
Height: 59.6 cm
Richard Breeze, London
Price: £385

nament. The tournament had been arranged by Lord Eglinton, who sincerely attempted to recreate the age of the fourteenth-century chronicler Jean Froissart in 1839.

The vast majority of Victorian pewter drinking vessels and measures were made to conform to the Imperial Standard Measures imposed in 1826, measures which were slightly more generous for wine than the Old English Wine measures, and marginally smaller for ale. In American pewter, however, the measures remained the same as the Old English Wine Standard, and have done to this day. In Britain, local makers were required to stamp their drinking

relatively restricted market at the beginning of the nineteenth century, but good, and indeed revolutionary, examples were included in J. C. Loudon's *Encyclopaedia of Cottage, Farm and Villa Architecture* of 1813, and in his *Encyclopaedia of Gardening*, published in 1828. This is one of

the earliest examples of furniture being made with interchangeable sections, so that a variety of different designs could be assembled from a limited number of prefabricated parts.

'An enfilade, or vista, through a modern house, is occasionally increased by a conservatory at one end, and repeated by a large mirror at the opposite end', wrote Humphrey Repton, architect and landscape gardener, in 1816. The owners of new Victorian houses took this suggestion to their hearts, and conservatories constructed with prefabricated sections from the Scottish ironworks of the Carron Company blossomed as adjuncts to many homes. The mighty ironworks of Coalbrookdale, in decline since the death of Edmund Darby in 1801, revived with astonishing speed in 1828, when his two sons Abraham and Alfred took over the running of the firm and entered en-

88   thusiastically into the manufacture of

Cast-iron boot scraper
Height: 17.1 cm
Sold: Christie's, Great Tew Park,
28/5/87
Price: £660

---

cast-iron furniture. At first the range was limited to use in the garden and conservatory, but soon manufacture extended to hallstands, umbrella stands, jardinières, and a catalogue of astonishing variety, which was proudly shown at the Great Exhibition in 1851.

There were two more revolutionary technical advances in iron and steel production, the Bessemer and Siemens-Martin processes in 1856 and 1865 respectively, which resulted in a great outpouring of decorative cast iron in every form imaginable, from faithful reproductions of Tudor firedogs and firebacks, cressets and grates, to doorstops and bootscrapers in the shape of 'Mr Punch', dogs, horses, cats and fleurs de lys. The new cast iron lacked the bloom and softness of the earlier material, either wrought or cast. In effect, it was mild steel, a hybrid from which knife blades and umbrella stands could be cast with equal ease. With no tradition to follow and every design in the book there for the taking, the metalworkers and ironfounders of the nineteenth century cannot be blamed for the abysmal standard of much of their output. As with early plastics, if the manufacturing techniques were there and the raw material could be made to comply, anything that could be made was made.

'PONTYPOOL' AND TOLEWARE

There is one small branch of the iron and steel industry which has its roots in eighteenth-century traditions and which, though it was pressed into service to make biscuit tins and commercial canisters, continued to make the most delightful articles with great taste. Tinplate, or toleware, was originally manufactured by John Hannay of Pontypool in 1720. So-called 'Pontypool' ware was, however, first made by John Payne of Bridgwater, near Bristol, in 1728. The term refers to thin sheets of iron coated with tin (tinplate) painted with black enamel and stoved – a process known as 'japanning' because it bears a superficial resemblance to lacquerware. The japanned tinplate was then painted and decorated with brightly coloured enamels, often with the addition of gilding, particularly in the nineteenth century. The finished article was then 'pickled' to give it a hard, high shine.

The most common Victorian japan-ned items to be found today are trays, often in graduated sets of three or four, and, most typically, decorated with 'chinoiserie'; scallop-edged *verrières* painted with landscapes, fruit, flowers or game; urns and chestnut urns; small, pierced-rim jardinières; pierced, shallow fruit baskets; and charming coalbins or boxes.

Continental *tole peinte*, as japan-ned toleware is known, tends to be more ornate and ambitious than British designs and in more classical styles, whereas American toleware often has stencilled decoration, and was used for more functional articles such as plate and dish warmers. In Pennsylvania there was a considerable output of toleware which has many characteristics in common with the painted and stencilled furniture made by the Dutch inhabitants of Pennsylvania.

Japanned coal box
Height: 55.8 cm
Sold: Christie's, Great Tew Park, 28/5/87
Price: £495

Object	Quality of manufacture	Quality of design and/or decoration	Rarity	Price (£)	Price ($)
Brass					
pair of andirons	8	8	■ ■	600–900	1140–1710
pair of bath taps	7	7	■ ■	50-100	95–190
pair of candlesticks	7	7	■	75–150	140–285
pair of doorstops	7	7	■ ■	75–150	140–285
lantern	6	7	■ ■	50–100	95–190
honesty box, double-lidded, press-button operated	7	6	■ ■ ■	400–800	760–1520
Copper					
kettle	6	7	■	50–100	95–190
saucepan and lid	7	7	■	50–100	95–190
dairy/preserving pan	7	7	■ ■	75–150	140–285
hot-water urn	7	7	■ ■ ■	100–250	190–475
lantern	8	7	■ ■	200–400	380–760
Iron					
cast-iron boot scraper	8	8	■ ■ ■	250–650	475–1235
cast-iron umbrella stand	7	7	■ ■	200–500	380–950
cast-iron cradle	7	6	■ ■ ■	300–500	570–950
cast-iron garden bench	7	7	■ ■	500–750	950–1425
wrought-iron weather vane	8	7	■ ■ ■	250–500	475–950
toleware coal box	8	7	■ ■ ■	250–500	475–950
Ormolu					
gilt-bronze lampstand	8	7	■ ■ ■	200–400	380–760

Qualities on a scale 1-10   ■ Rare   ■ ■ Very rare   ■ ■ ■ Extremely rare

Object	Quality of manufacture	Quality of design and/or decoration	Rarity	Price (£)	Price ($)
Pewter					
pair of candlesticks	7	6	■ ■	40–80	75–150
charger	7	7	■	50–100	95–190
biscuit barrel by Liberty	7	8	■ ■	200–400	380–760
pair of pepper pots	7	7	■ ■	40–80	75–150
set of four quart mugs	7	6	■ ■	100–200	190–380
set of seven measures	7	6	■ ■ ■	150–300	285–570
set of four conical measures by Fothergills	7	6	■ ■ ■	300–500	570–950
pair of entrée dishes and covers	7	7	■ ■	200–400	380–760

Qualities on a scale 1-10   ■ Rare   ■ ■ Very rare   ■ ■ ■ Extremely rare

Object	Quality of manufacture	Quality of design and/or decoration	Rarity	Price (£)	Price ($)
Silver					
pair of salt cellars	7	7	■ ■	200–500	380–950
pair of candlesticks	7	6	■	150–350	285–665
kettle on stand	7	7	■ ■	300–500	570–950
christening mug by J. & J. Angell	8	7	■ ■ ■	150–250	285–475
cake basket	8	7	■ ■ ■	400–500	760–950
rose bowl by J. Dixon & Co.	8	6	■ ■	400–500	760–950
snuff box	7	7	■	250–500	475–950
vinaigrette	7	6	■	200–400	380–760
fish slice and serving fork	7	7	■ ■	100–300	190–570
pair of sugar tongs	7	6	■ ■	75–150	140–285
caddy spoon	7	7	■	100–200	190–380
water jug	8	7	■ ■	200–400	380–760
salver by Walker & Hall	7	6	■ ■	100–200	190–380
three-piece coffee service	7	6	■ ■	400–600	760–1140
three-piece tea service by Stephen Smith	8	7	■ ■ ■	800–1000+	1520–1900+
water jug with engraved decoration by Stephen Smith	8	7	■ ■	500–750	950–1425
silver-mounted glass claret jug by W. & G. Sissons	8	6	■ ■	500–750	950–1425
silver-mounted glass claret jug (maker unknown)	7	6	■ ■	250–600	475–1140
parcel-gilt cup by Henry Bourne	8	6	■ ■	350–500	665–950
parcel-gilt decanter stand by Tiffany & Co.	8	6	■ ■	800–1000+	1520–1900+
coffee pot by Edward Barnard & Co.	7	7	■ ■	400–600	760–1140
tea caddy by Hunt & Roskell	8	8	■ ■ ■	400–600	760–1140
pair of sugar casters	7	6	■ ■	250–500	475–950
sugar caster in the form of an owl	7	7	■ ■ ■	600–900	1140–1710
sugar caster in the form of a cat/dog	7	6	■ ■	250–350	475–665
mustard pot	7	6	■ ■	200–400	380–760

Qualities on a scale 1-10   ■ Rare   ■ ■ Very rare   ■ ■ ■ Extremely rare

Object	Quality of manufacture	Quality of design and/or decoration	Rarity	Price (£)	Price ($)
cruet frame	7	6	■ ■	100–300	190–570
silver-mounted glass biscuit jar	7	6	■	200–400	380–760
set of four parcel-gilt menu holders	8	6	■ ■	150–450	285–855
silver-mounted mirror frame	7	7	■	250–500	475–950
cake basket by Henry Wilkinson & Son	7	6	■ ■	500–700	950–1330
set of twelve dinner forks by Tiffany & Co.	8	7	■ ■ ■	800–1000	1520–1900
cheroot case decorated with enamels	7	7	■ ■	250–500	475–950

Silver plate

Object	Quality of manufacture	Quality of design and/or decoration	Rarity	Price (£)	Price ($)
stationery box by Elkington's	8	7	■ ■	500–750	950–1425
five-piece tea and coffee service	7	7	■	400–600	760–1140
soup tureen and cover by Elkington's	8	6	■ ■	100–200	190–380
tea urn	7	6	■ ■	150–250	285–475
biscuit barrel	7	6	■	60–120	115–230
'Aesthetic'-style card case	7	7	■ ■	50–100	95–190
serving tray	7	6	■	100–300	190–570
Sheffield plate wine wagon	8	7	■ ■ ■	550–700	1045–1330
pair of two-light candelabra	6	6	■ ■	200–400	380–760
Sheffield plate four-branch epergne	8	8	■ ■ ■	800–1000+	1520–1900+
kettle on stand	7	6	■	200–400	380–760
pair of Sheffield plate candlesticks	7	7	■ ■	200–500	380–950
cruet frame (with seven cut-glass condiment bottles)	7	6	■ ■	100–200	190–380
three-footed salver, decorated in rococo style	6	6	■	100–200	190–380
two-handled gallery teatray	7	6	■ ■	150–300	285–570
pair of entrée dishes with two-handled covers	7	7	■ ■	150–300	285–570

Qualities on a scale 1-10   ■ Rare   ■ ■ Very rare   ■ ■ ■ Extremely rare

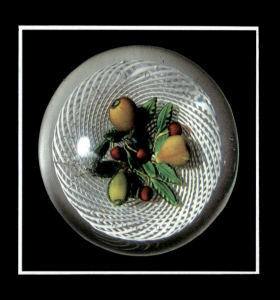

CHAPTER FIVE

GLASS

St Louis paperweight
Diameter: 8 cm
Sold: Phillips, London, 10/6/87
Price: £484

In 1745 a heavy excise duty was imposed on glass in England, because of the enormous quantity of glass used for windows. Indeed, at one time England suffered a direct Window Tax, which resulted in some house-owners bricking up unnecessary windows in order to save money. Great quantities of glass were also used for making bottles for beer and wines. The excise duty on the glass turned out to be such a lucrative source of funding for wars and the national economy that it was not lifted until 1845.

In England coloured and opaque white glass were developed from necessity, since both were exempt

Cased pink glass vase with gilt decoration
Height: 16.8 cm
Jeanette Hayhurst, London
Price: £120

from tax. But even with these forms of glass the hands of the English glassmakers were tied. They were not free to experiment to make a 'pot of metal' and try out new methods of manufacture, for the tax was imposed on the weight of the metal in the pot. (In its molten state, glass is a metal, albeit with very different properties from all the others.)

Much of the glass produced in the nineteenth century was a reproduction of sixteenth- and seventeenth-century glass, known as 'soda glass'. It has an uneven quality, a slightly yellow or green tinge, and traces of bubbling. 'Flint glass' or crystal glass was also made; this is completely pure and colourless, and has a metallic sound when it is struck.

NEWCASTLE, GATESHEAD AND AMERICA

In spite of the restrictions on glass production, by the end of the eighteenth century the glasshouses in and around Tyneside, the Midlands and the north-east of England were producing enormous quantities of uncoloured drinking glasses. Shiploads of 'Newcastle glass' were exported to America, undercutting the prices of the infant American industry which was struggling to get on its feet. This made the American glassmakers extremely angry, and in 1829 they reported the matter to the Commissioners of Excise: 'Our correspondent in New York lately advised us that the market for flint Glass in that City, is destroyed by Importations from *Newcastle*, made almost entirely from the Gateshead Works in that place and expresses his utter astonishment how they can possibly sell Goods at a *third of the value* which would remunerate others. It is very evident there is only one way that this can be done to *any advantage* on their part – viz; by defrauding the Revenue.' The report stated that the exports from the Tyne were immense and advised the Commissioners 'to have an *eye* on the officers *employed at the works'*. The chief culprit in this extremely lucrative export trade was the Sowerby Glassworks at Gateshead on the Tyne, a company which was to become a household name in the nineteenth century.

The precise details of the shapes and patterns of domestic glass shipped to America are not known, but between 1826 and 1833 the Sowerby Glassworks exported several thou-

American green glass vase with silver overlay
Height: 31.7 cm
Sold: Phillips, London, 24/3/87
Price: £462

**Bohemian 'Mary Gregory'
style vase**
Height: 27.6 cm
Sold: Phillips, London, 11/3/87
Price: £682

sand hundredweight across the Atlantic – all produced by traditional methods of glassmaking: bowls were blown or blow-moulded, stems and feet were handmade – all that had changed was the quantity of raw metal. The ingredients could now be ground by machine and the furnaces heated more efficiently with coke; steam-driven lathes could cut, grind, and polish glass to a high finish, processes which had been done by

hand until the end of the eighteenth century.

PRESS-MOULDED GLASS

There were very few glassworks in America at the beginning of the nineteenth century – perhaps no more than a dozen. The urgent need to manufacture domestic glassware of all sorts on a gigantic scale was all too evident, however, and in the 1820s several skilled glassworkers with considerable technical ability were working on the problem. Deming Jarves of the New England Glass Company, Cambridge, Mass. left to found a rival firm, the Boston and Sandwich Company, near Cape Cod, and began experimenting with an ancient, near-forgotten process of press-moulding glass. Enoch Robinson, a carpenter by trade, introduced the first machine for pressing glass at the New England Glass Company Works in 1827. Soon after, Jarves installed an improved version in his factory, and press-moulded glass began to be made in great quantities.

The next few years saw a dozen more patents taken out in America for press-moulding machines, and a series of designs created specially for press-moulding techniques. Intricate surface patterns could be incorporated into the metal mould for relatively little extra cost; one of the most popular was a geometrical lacy pattern which was used in hundreds of different variations on plates, cup-plates and shallow dishes. Press-moulding allowed bottles, decanters, jugs, goblets and candlesticks to be ribbed, fluted, beaded and patterned in one operation. It was an incredible saving in cost, and in America, where there was no excise tax, was exploited to the full.

Bohemian decanter, cut and overlaid
Height: 40.4 cm
Sold: Phillips, London, 11/3/87
Price: £605

A great deal of heavy cut-glass and lustres for chandeliers, as well as a fair amount of domestic glass, was made in Ireland, duty-free and easily accessible to the English glassmakers, many of whom had left to establish more profitable factories in and around Waterford in the second half of the eighteenth century. While this source of supply was available, press-moulded glass held no particular attraction for English glassmakers. But in 1825 the British government imposed an excise tax on glass in Ireland, and in the next few years, as the American press-moulded output grew, the Irish export market

Press-moulded vase
Height: 22.2 cm
Jeanette Hayhurst, London
Price: £68

was clearly under threat. The first press-moulding machine was installed in a Birmingham glasshouse in 1831, and shortly afterwards others were being used in Stourbridge in the Midlands, the traditional centre for glassmaking in England. Among the earliest items to be made in any quantity were pressed-glass salt cellars – the swingeing tax on salt was lifted in 1835, cutting the price by ninety per cent.

BOHEMIAN GLASS

On the whole, pressed glass was considered suitable only for 'common

Bohemian cut-glass vase
Height: 35.8 cm
Sold: Bearne's, Torquay, 8/7/85
Price (pair): £814

and cheap articles', by the English purists. They said that the process resulted in glass which 'lacked the brilliant transparency so admired in cut glass'. Instead, envious eyes turned towards Germany, Bohemia and Czechoslovakia, which had for centuries made some of the finest glass in Europe. Their industry had suffered severely during the Napoleonic Wars, but after 1815 it made a spectacular revival. Bohemian glassworkers had always been supreme in the arts of cutting and engraving, and at the beginning of the nineteenth century they surpassed themselves. Two radically new forms of glass emerged, which may well have been influenced by Wedgwood's black basaltes and marbled clay: Hyalith, which was a black glass decorated in silver or gold, often with designs taken from Oriental lacquer, and Lithyalin, which resembled marble agate and striated stone. Both were manufactured from about 1828 onwards.

CASED GLASS, OPALINE AND CUT GLASS

The Bohemian technique of making ruby glass was infinitely superior to any other: because clear glass could not be stained red, it was 'cased', or dipped, to achieve a uniform colour, unlike 'stained glass' which was tinted right through. When more than one colour is layered over ruby red, it is known as 'overlaid' glass.

The technique of layering glass in different colours and then cutting it away to the clear body caught the Victorian eye. Called 'flashed glass', it was at its most effective (or so the Victorians thought) when an opaque white glass was layered over rich ruby red glass (preferably Bohemian)

tween the early 1830s and 1845, when the excise duty was finally lifted. Cut glass continued to be greatly in demand, and through a combination of the growing love of surface ornament and the economic necessity of reducing the amount of raw material, the cutting became wilder and more profligate, frequently covering the entire surface with geometric, largely machine-cut patterns. It was this trend that led John Ruskin to declare that 'all cut glass is barbarous'.

Between 1845 and 1851, the year of the Great Exhibition, both the English and the American glass industries had made great strides in production techniques and methods

White cased glass goblet
Height: 19.4 cm
Jeanette Hayhurst, London
Price: £130

and then cut away and enamel-painted with swags of fruit and flowers.

Because of the tax on glass, many English glasshouses, Sowerby included, found themselves in considerable financial difficulties be-

Transparentmalerei **beaker**
Height: 14.2 cm
Sold: Phillips, London, 11/3/87
Price: £462

101

of decoration. The Stourbridge firm founded by Benjamin Richardson had been making opaline glass since the 1840s, decorated in the fashionable manner, with classical figures, Greek key pattern and anthemion, and painted in terracotta and gilt in a manner reminiscent of Wedgwood's 'Etruscan' ware. Thomas Webb made a similar version, much of it painted by Thomas Battam, who decorated terracotta vases and urns for Blanchard & Co., and Benjamin Richardson, then manager of T. Hawkes & Co. of Birmingham, first to install a machine for press-moulded glass, was making flashed and cased glass in the Bohemian manner in 1845.

In America, the New England Glass Company was making 'richly coloured and decorated glassware . . . so much admired under the name of 'Bohemian glass'.' Towards the end of the century the inspiration for another range of Bohemian glass was poached by an enterprising glass decorator from the Boston & Sandwich Glass Company, Mary Gregory. Cheaply made jugs, decanters, vases and glasses from Bohemia, decorated in white enamel with children at play, were becoming extremely popular with the American market, and Mary Gregory copied some of this glass. Since then she has inaccurately been credited with the origination of the whole range, which is now widely known as 'Mary Gregory glass'. The press-moulded glass industry was producing quantities of 'tortoiseshell' and marbled glass, mainly 'slag glass' in purple and white, or, to use its more dignified name, Lithyalin.

An exhibition was held in Birmingham in 1849. Among the exhibits were Rice Harris & Sons' examples of drinking glasses, tumblers, salt cellars and sugar bowls, press-moulded in patterns of cut glass, and polished and finished so that they had 'a degree of sharpness in all the ornamental parts, which render it difficult without a closer examination to say whether or not they have been subjected to the operation of the glass cutter's wheel'.

CRYSTAL

Up to the 1860s clear crystal table glass was, in the main, made in shapes derived from classical forms, engraved with anthemion, Greek key and formal Greek ornament. In the

Baccarat paperweight with sulphide of Queen Victoria
Diameter: 8.8 cm
Sold: Phillips, London, 10/6/87
Price: £572

1850s the Stourbridge firm of Richardson's had begun to use acid-etching rather than engraving to achieve the same results but at less cost, and by 1865 geometric etching was being done by machines. There was a spate of fern decoration on glass (as well as on ceramics, silver, printed cottons and cast-iron garden furniture) from the 1850s onwards, probably related to the publication of John Moore's *Ferns of Great Britain and Ireland* in 1855. Crystal drinking glasses were very thinly blown, with straw-thin stems, and the old champagne flute was replaced by the shallow goblet shape.

FAÇON DE VENISE AND AESTHETIC GLASS

Glass had not yet been brought into line with the all-pervading Medieval and Romantic fashions that prevailed in this period, but it was not long before this was put right. The remedy lay in surviving examples of early Venetian glass. 'Façon de Venise' was made at first by Powell's of Whitefriars, with the benediction of William Morris, and was soon being copied by glassmakers up and down the country as they climbed on the Medieval bandwagon. The best examples were handmade, from the old formula 'soda glass' with its green or yellow tinge, with the twisted handles authentically pincered, the threading applied by hand. Dr Antonio Salviati, founder of the Venice and Murano Glass Company in 1868, opened showrooms in St James's Street full of 'Venetian Renaissance' glass of every kind.

Inevitably, copies with varying degrees of inaccuracy were made by the large glass companies. Tinted 'flint' glass, less amenable to pincering and 103

Façon de Venise stemmed vessel
Height: 16.4 cm
Jeanette Hayhurst, London
Price: £195

the studio, or on the sideboards of the wealthy, but for aught else it is entirely useless.'

Two years later, at the Paris Exhibition, Powell's glass came under fire. 'One gets tired of the constant repetition of a Venetian goblet, a Venetian vase, a Venetian jug, as if nothing else in the world could be made', wrote a critical observer. 'Let us hope that this firm will yet find out a purer field of activity than the Venetian.' As it happened, this was precisely what Powell's of White-

Façon de Venise drinking glass
Height: 12.3 cm
Jeanette Hayhurst, London
Price: £110

threading, twisting and looping, was used to make inelegant pastiches. By 1876 there were machines to do the threading, which was uniform and dull, and in several cases the colour of the glass was a rather nasty watercolour khaki. But even Dr Salviati's finest examples failed to impress practical, working glassmakers. In his report to the Society of Arts on the Paris Exhibition of 1876, a Mr T. J. Wilkinson wrote: 'The greatest display...is made by Dr Salviati of Venice...the works displayed here are as odd-looking and as grotesque in their appearance as we should consider any number of men who thought fit to dress themselves in the habiliments of the Middle Ages; that being the era the glass is supposed to be a copy of. All very well to put in

friars was in the process of doing. From about 1861, the architect Philip Webb had been designing a limited range of glass in the Aesthetic manner for Powell's which, for purity of form, has probably not been excelled. Totally free of ornament, except perhaps for a row of stylized 'raspberry prunts', the designs were stripped to the bone, without engraving, cutting, or etching. It was a form imitated with some success by Sowerby, who brought a small number of glassblowers to England from Italy to help in the endeavour.

'THE AGE OF PLAIN GLASS IS GONE OR GOING'

The plain, undecorated appearance of 'Aesthetic glass' drew a mixed response from the general buying public. While hailed by Mrs Loftie, writing in *Art at Home* in 1878, as being a great improvement on the 'cast and moulded atrocities which have hitherto monopolized the cheap market', *The Pottery Gazette* thought otherwise. This trade magazine roundly condemned 'the present flimsy glass that decorates our tables, such as etched, spun, twisted, Venetian and other abortions that meet us at nearly every dinner table'. The same magazine asked: 'Where is the brilliant cut glass that used to set off our silver and our damask cloth? Gone. I fear it has given way to the fashion of the age – the flimsy fashion of 1879.' A few years later, the same publication was exultant. In 1882 it reported gleefully that 'the age of plain glass is gone or going, and good cut and engraved glass is fast coming in again'.

The great British public was not very interested in these Aesthetic debates. For them there was a mul-

titude of wonderful things to choose from, and all of them made in glass. From the 1850s onwards there were thick, pressed-glass celery vases with sand-blasted matt decoration, sometimes broken with cut-glass designs. By the 1870s there were matt-finished models of Landseer's lions in

Silver-mounted claret jug
Height: 25.6 cm
Sold: Christie's, Scotland, 11/11/87
Price: £682

Trafalgar Square, and small vessels in the form of hands to hold trinkets. There were all kinds of 'novelties' in what is called 'Nailsea' glass – made in Nailsea in the eighteenth century but mainly in Warrington and Gateshead during the nineteenth – and clear pressed-glass commemorative and fancy plates, dishes, bowls and trinket trays. The Great Exhibition displayed ranges of coloured glass in blue, opal-coated blue, pearl opal, frosted opal, ruby, black, pale green,

Vaseline glass ornament
Height: 10 cm
Jeanette Hayhurst, London
Price: £135

dark green, turquoise, and a multitude of others.

In the 1870s, keeping abreast of the general fashion trends, the glasshouses of the north-east of England began to make 'green malachite', 'brown malachite', and the purple and white 'slag glass' that had originated in Bohemia in the 1820s as 'Lithyalin', all in the fashionable 'archaeological' manner. Most of the objects were confined to the plainer shapes such as spill vases and simple novelties. Opaque white 'Vitroporcelain' and Sowerby's 'Patent Queen's Ivory' followed in the 1880s in pressed patterns, some of them taken from Walter Crane's illustrations, others based on simple 'daisy chain' designs.

PEACH BLOW AND QUEEN'S BURMESE

Several glasshouses in America and England were experimenting with shaded body colours in the 1880s. The New England Glass Works produced a colour called 'Amberina' in 1883 and later developed a matt-finish glass which was shaded from cream to rose, yellow to pink or from blue to pink. Also in 1883, Walsh of Birmingham produced their 'Sunrise' range and, at much the same time, the Mount Washington Glass Company produced a very similar product which they called 'Burmese' and which was shaded from rose-pink to cream-yellow. Queen Victoria was sent some examples of this blushing glass, for which she paid the considerable sum of £250. Thomas Webb of Stourbridge promptly obtained a licence to manufacture it, and named it 'Queen's Burmese'.

In March 1886, a Chinese porcelain vase from the estate of Mrs Mary

Carnival glass dish
Height: 6 cm
Jeanette Hayhurst, London
Price: £35

of the fashion, the American firm of Hobbs, Brockunier and Co. of West Virginia made copies in glass of the famous Chinese porcelain.

FIN DE SIÈCLE FANTASIES

There were two developments which bracket the popular market at one end and the exclusive at the other. 'Blue Pearline' glass, made by Sowerby's in 1889 and generally called 'vaseline' glass because of its curious petroleum-like appearance, stands at the 'novelty' end, while at the other end is Tiffany's 'Favrile' iridescent glass and that produced by Gallé and Loetz (although they hardly fall within the category of Victoriana). In between these two extremes, the one used for pressed-glass novelties and the other for expensive, naturalistic vases in the shape of flowers, is all the opalescent and mother-of-pearl glass that went into those genteel and astounding table centrepieces that were an obligatory decoration at a dinner party at the end of the nineteenth century.

Morgan was sold for $18,000 by the American Art Galleries, New York. It was described in the catalogue as having the most exquisite glaze, 'peach-blow' in colour, and precipitated a fashion in America for 'peach blow' complexions with the assistance of 'peach blow' face powders, lipsticks and beauty aids. The New England Glass Company called their shaded glass 'Peach Glass' following this craze. Soon after the beginning

Cranberry glass centrepiece
Height: 52 cm
Jeanette Hayhurst, London
Price: £450

Object	Quality of manufacture	Quality of design and/or decoration	Rarity	Price (£)	Price ($)
Beakers					
transparentmalerei	8	7	■ ■	300–600	570–1140
pressed glass by Sowerby's	6	7	■	30–60	55–115
Bohemian amber-flash with engraved panels	8	7	■ ■ ■	200–300	380–570
Bottles					
'Nailsea'-style flask	7	7	■ ■	100–200	190–380
silver-mounted cut-glass scent bottle	7	6	■	65–130	125–250
square spirit bottles with cut decoration (set of three)	7	6	■ ■	200–400	380–760
Bowls					
Baccarat engraved	8	7	■ ■	300–800	570–1520
façon de Venise	8	7	■ ■	120–240	230–455
tazza with turquoise enamelling	6	6	■	75–150	140–285
Irish cut-glass fruit bowl	8	7	■ ■	500–1000	950–1900
French enamelled tazza	8	7	■ ■	300–600	380–1140
Decanters					
Bohemian cased and etched	8	7	■ ■	100–500	190–950
cut glass	7	7	■	100–300	190–570
geometric slice-cut heavy glass	7	6	■ ■	400–800	760–1520
pair of Scottish decanters with engraved thistles	7	7	■ ■ ■	200–400	380–760
pair of decanters with facet-cut necks	7	6	■ ■	150–300	285–570
carafe with acid-etched decoration	7	7	■	60–120	115–230
engraved decanter with barley-twist handle	7	6	■ ■ ■	150–250	285–475
pair of ship's decanters and stoppers	7	7	■	100–300	190–380
pair of hobnail-cut claret decanters and stoppers	7	6	■ ■	250–500	475–950

Qualities on a scale 1-10   ■ Rare   ■ ■ Very rare   ■ ■ ■ Extremely rare

Object	Quality of manufacture	Quality of design and/or decoration	Rarity	Price (£)	Price ($)
Dishes					
carnival glass	6	6	■	25–75	45–140
pressed glass by Sowerby's	6	7	■	30–60	55–15
Drinking glasses					
façon de Venise	8	7	■ ■	75–150	140–285
white cased goblet	7	6	■ ■	80–160	150–305
champagne glasses with overlay and faceted stems (set of eight)	7	7	■ ■	200–300	380–570
engraved ruby goblet on baluster stem	7	6	■	60–120	115–230
Bohemian ruby and green glass with amber border	8	8	■ ■ ■	500–750	950–1425
Bohemian amber-flashed engraved goblet	8	7	■ ■	300–600	570–1140
pair of French opaline glasses	8	7	■ ■	450–650	855–1235
Jugs					
silver-mounted claret jug	7	7	■	300–700	570–1330
'Nailsea'-style turquoise glass with pulled white thread decoration	7	7	■ ■	200–400	380–760
claret jug with Greek key cutting	7	6	■ ■	100–200	190–380
cut and engraved celery jug	7	7	■	50–100	95–190
Bohemian ruby-flash faceted and gilt cream jug	8	7	■ ■ ■	100–200	190–380
Miscellaneous					
Bohemian gilt Hyalith preserve pot and cover	7	7	■ ■	300–600	570–1140
cut-glass honey jar and cover	7	6	■	150–300	285–570
Bohemian enamelled and gilt urn and pedestal	7	7	■ ■	400–800	760–1520
pair of heavy cut-glass jars, covers and stands	6	6	■ ■	450–700	855–1330

Qualities on a scale 1-10   ■ Rare   ■ ■ Very rare   ■ ■ ■ Extremely rare

Object	Quality of manufacture	Quality of design and/or decoration	Rarity	Price (£)	Price ($)
Ornaments					
cranberry glass centrepiece	7	6	■ ■	400–600	760–1140
Vaseline glass ornament	7	6	■ ■	80–200	150–380
ruby glass bell with clear handle	7	6	■ ■	75–150	140–285
pair of candlesticks with gilt panels and cut prismatic drops	7	5	■ ■	300–500	570–950
glass domed model of a ship in clear and opaque coloured and spun glass	8	7	■ ■	150–300	285–570
centrepiece with silver feet	8	6	■ ■	550–900	1045–1710
French cut-glass and gilt-bronze mounted three-piece garniture	7	7	■ ■ ■	800–1000+	1520–1900+
Bohemian cameo centrepiece	8	7	■ ■	400–800	760–1520
Paperweights					
Baccarat faceted sulphide	8	7	■ ■	400–700	760–1330
Baccarat faceted millefiori mushroom	8	7	■ ■	600–1000+	1140–1900+
Clichy three-colour spiral	8	8	■ ■	750–1000+	1425–1900+
St Louis fruit and latticino	8	7	■ ■	300–600	570–1140
New England fruit	7	7	■ ■	200–400	380–760
Clichy pansy	8	7	■ ■	500–750	950–1425
St Louis miniature fruit	8	7	■ ■	400–600	760–1140
St Louis miniature three-coloured crown	8	7	■ ■ ■	450–650	855–1235
St Louis millefiori mushroom	8	7	■ ■ ■	800–1000+	1520–1900+

Qualities on a scale 1-10   ■ Rare   ■ ■ Very rare   ■ ■ ■ Extremely rare

Object	Quality of manufacture	Quality of design and/or decoration	Rarity	Price (£)	Price ($)
Vases					
cased pink glass with gilt decoration	6	6	■ ■	75–150	140–285
American green glass with silver overlay	7	7	■ ■ ■	300–700	570–1330
press-moulded	6	6	■	40–120	75–230
Bohemian cut glass	7	7	■ ■	250–500	475–950
slag glass spill vase	7	6	■ ■	30–60	55–115
pair of Bohemian 'Mary Gregory'-style ruby glass vases	8	7	■ ■ ■	500–900	950–1710
Bohemian engraved ruby-flash	8	7	■ ■	300–600	570–1140
Bohemian heavy cut glass	8	8	■ ■ ■	500–1000	950–1900
Bohemian enamelled and gilt cranberry vase	8	7	■ ■	200–400	380–760
cameo vase by Stevens & Williams	8	7	■ ■	500–1000+	950–1900+

Qualities on a scale 1-10   ■ Rare   ■ ■ Very rare   ■ ■ ■ Extremely rare   111

CHAPTER SIX

DECORATIVE
OBJECTS

Russian (Lukutin) lacquered box
12.5 × 17.5 cm
Sold: Phillips, London, 17/11/87
Price: £198

**French plaster reduction of the
Venus de Milo**
Height: 117.8 cm
Sold: Christie's, Great Tew Park,
28/5/87
Price: £418

Eighteenth-century paintings and portraits which depict the interiors of houses of the time give an idea of how sparsely furnished most rooms were. What a contrast they are to nineteenth-century interiors, which are swamped with useless decorative objects of all sorts. Confronted by so much ornament, so many *objets d'art* which grew and multiplied throughout the nineteenth century, it is reassuring to discover that many Victorians were fully aware that the plethora of revivals, reproductions, copies and original work was not only confusing, but also not conducive to an appreciation of either Art or Beauty. Mrs Haweis, that bold adviser on such matters, says as much. 'We have *too much* art now – too much and too poor – the result of competition, want of leisure, avidity of demand for cheap production, and too great a sub-division of labour.' She has stated the problem in a nutshell, and goes on to advocate the choice of 'old work', delivering a homily on the craftsmanship of those who have gone before.

'OLD WORK' IS BEST

'In using the wide term "old work"', she writes, 'I am speaking chiefly of medieval work, and of that chiefly English, though much that I say applies to all Europe, old Greece, Etruria, Egypt, or India. I find the most feeling and most striving for truth between the thirteenth and sixteenth centuries, most knowledge with waning fervour between the sixteenth and eighteenth, starting from Raffaelle, and the bathos (speaking generally) between the middle of the eighteenth and nineteenth centuries.'

Taste, then, it seems, must be guided by moral principles and not

Marble and gilt metal mantel clock
Height: 46.2 cm
Sold: Christie's, Scotland, 11/10/87
Price: £462

Marble figure of Apollo
Height: 103.7 cm
Sold: Phillips, London, 14/4/87
Price: £682

necessarily by form and beauty. Mrs Haweis makes this clear in her catalogue of 'old works' which notably excludes the Romans. Unlike the Greeks, she avers, who were ennobled by the worship of the Beautiful, Roman art 'aimed simply at the glorification of self, and was debased proportionately.'

It seems, today, an extraordinary viewpoint, but perhaps it explains the rising tide of clutter among the middle classes, which reached its height in the 1880s. If one lived surrounded by 'things of beauty' then by some peculiar osmosis one could

absorb the beauty into one's life and thus be raised to a higher moral plane. The dilemma of *too much*, however, remained. 'What', asks Mrs Haweis, 'are we to do?' After discoursing at length on the South Kensington School of Design (to which had been added a museum, now the Victoria and Albert Museum) and all the other institutions expressly set up to help educate people about art, which she largely dismisses, she ends by letting her readers down with a bump. 'In dress, in home-adornment, in every department of art — regardless of derision, censure, and advice – WE MUST DO AS WE LIKE.'

Indian silvered filigree urn and cover
Height: 47.7 cm
Sold: Christie's, Great Tew Park, 28/5/87
Price: £264

No suggestion that a 'Grecian' vase was not really suitable for a 'medieval' hall, or that machine-made tapestry might not be the best thing to hang on the walls of an 'Adam' parlour, or that a diminutive Parian Venus de Milo might look a little absurd on top of a whatnot.

In order to hack a way through the undergrowth of mass production, one must turn elsewhere for the lines that broadly influenced the better manufacturers to make one particular style for the mass market rather than another. They were, inevitably, to reproduce what had been high fashion for the discriminating in the recent past.

RUNNING IN DECORATIVE CIRCLES

The aristocracy, the 'old money', whose houses had stood for centuries had, down the years, added more rooms, corridors and passages to their homes; each style of interior decoration could therefore be accommodated at the same time, more often than not, in newly built rooms of the appropriate proportions. But the entrepreneurs of the Industrial Revolution, the 'new money', built larger, more spectacular and more splendid rooms to demonstrate their power and position. The large sizes of these rooms were not designed for the neo-classical style and sparse furnishings advocated by Adam and his followers well into the nineteenth century, and so the need arose for large, elaborate pieces of furniture. There was another reason for this furniture – it was needed to display the Wedgwood jasperware, the Etruscan ware, and the collections of Sèvres and Dresden that the new money bought.

At the beginning of the century, a small boudoir of impeccable rococo taste, such as the room in Count Mnischek's house in Paris, described in the *Petite Revue* of 1864, consisted of a well-proportioned room, 'entirely faced with mirrors on which gold arabesques scroll and form

Pair of gilt bronze Empire-style ewers
Height: 37.2 cm
Sold: Phillips, London, 28/4/87
Price: £935

brackets that support a collection of Dresden china, the reflection of which doubles the magical effect. A clock and sconces of Dresden complete the harmonious image.' How could such a restrained and understated room satisfy a man with a new position in society? His collection of Dresden was far too large to be displayed on a few gilded brackets, and if it was displayed behind the fretted glass doors of a china cabinet, how could it be seen? He needed decorative shelves, large-paned glass-fronted cabinets, and several occasional tables on which to spread out all his possessions for daily admiration by his guests.

Once there was a market for decorative shelves, the furniture manufacturers decided that there was a need for them to be incorporated in

117

Hanging shelves in beech
Height: 84.7 cm
Sold: Christie's, Great Tew Park,
28/5/87
Price: £935

the houses that were in the process of being built all over the country. The shelves themselves generated a demand to be filled, and so the merry-go-round began, which was to continue throughout the nineteenth century. With each change in taste, there were new 'things of Beauty' to add to the collection – until every room was filled with decorative objects, every mantelpiece had its garniture reflected in an overmantel mirror, every hall and conservatory had its jardinière and plant stand, every dining table, sideboard and chiffonier was overloaded with comports, tazzas, trophies and centrepieces, as well as candlesticks, vases, photographs in frames and other ornaments or bric-à-brac.

LITTLE BOXES

Individually, as is the case with a great deal of Victoriana, many of the pieces which were displayed were remarkably well made and designed, particularly those that were produced by relatively small manufacturers, who retained an eighteenth-century sense of pride in their work. For example, in the hands of the big furniture manufacturing companies, veneer became no more than a cheap way of giving an apparently rich gloss to poor timber, but when it was used to decorate small boxes, as in Tunbridge ware, it could be transformed into a craft in itself.

Originally made as far back as the seventeenth century in thick, hand-cut veneers, Tunbridge ware was among the early examples of a souvenir trade – the Tunbridge Wells were a popular watering place. By the nineteenth century, Tunbridge ware had expanded to include all manner of small decorative objects, from tea caddies to the tops of small tables. It was no longer made in the

Walnut brass-bound writing slope
Height: 19.8 cm
McIntosh of Stockcross, Newbury
Price: £600

Brass casket with inset malachite bosses
Height: 27.2 cm
Wakelin & Linfield, Petworth
Price: £650

way that old-fashioned marquetry was, but in blocks of parquetry and with simpler patterns, fitted and glued together vertically. The blocks were then sliced horizontally, to provide identical tops and sides for a dozen or more boxes and tea caddies. Tunbridge ware was made by mechanical methods, yet it has an appeal and style entirely its own.

Perhaps it was the *pietra dura* inlays from Florence that encouraged the makers of Tunbridge ware to begin making far more intricate work, or perhaps it was the Italian 'souvenir' mosaics, but the same 'block' technique was used to make inlaid landscapes with borders of flowers and leaves, pictorial scenes and flower decoration. There are many people who decry what they term 'mass-produced decorative sheet veneers', but this ware took a great deal of skill and craftsmanship to produce. The vertical pieces of the design had to be cut out of different-coloured woods, cut precisely on the grain and fashioned into strips no thicker than a matchstick; then each tiny section was glued into the block. Finally the block itself had to be immaculately sliced horizontally across the end-grain and the sheet itself glued to the carcase of the box. 119

CASKETS AND WRITING BOXES

Caskets were also inordinately popular, either for locking away trinkets and jewellery, or as 'Medieval' pieces to place around an oak-panelled room. Many of these are well-proportioned, generally made in brass with little architectural features and details and set with polished striated agate or malachite bosses. The heavy, machine-carved 'Bible boxes' of the same period, however, made from artificially seasoned oak pegged together with uniform pegs, generally lack charm, even though some of them may incorporate a panel or part of a panel of genuine Tudor oak.

Writing boxes, stationery boxes and 'lap desks' proliferated in the nineteenth century with the introduction of the 'penny post' in 1840. Many were made in brass-bound mahogany or rosewood in miniature versions of

> **Olivewood games box, brass mounts inset with agate**
> Height: 11 cm
> Wakelin & Linfield, Petworth
> Price: £550

campaign chests, travelling military furniture which had been used during the Peninsular War of 1808-14. The style was too plain and functional to be appreciated early in the century, but during the Crimean Wars in 1854 it became widely popular for patriotic reasons.

Brass was also used for boxes and other objects in machine-made boulle-work. Boulle-work was originally an extremely rich and rare form of tortoiseshell inlaid with silver, but the nineteenth-century version was made by machine-grooving an intricate design usually into rosewood, and then pouring molten brass into the grooves to simulate inlay. This technique was also used for simulated damascening, or inlay, on inkstands and writing accessories, using cast steel and brass. Brass also appeared in the form of ormolu, mass-produced gilded cast brass, everywhere, from the heavy feet of rococo caskets to the imposing mounts and decoration of clocks and garnitures.

PAPIER MÂCHÉ AND PENWORK

Up to the middle of the eighteenth century, when the Adam brothers invented and patented a composition base to use for decorative plasterwork, architectural decoration had been made from papier mâché. In 1772 Henry Clay produced and patented a form of papier mâché which was hard, glossy, and could be cut and finished almost like wood. It was used first for making coach doors and panels, but it was so strong that soon it was being used to make trays and even table-tops. In 1816, Clay's business was taken over by Jennens & Bettridge, the best-known makers of nineteenth-century papier mâché ware. Another contender entered the field in 1830, when

Jackson & Sons began making a durable papier mâché called 'carton pierre', using a process from France.

Gilded, inlaid or painted, black lacquer on wood and papier mâché came and went as fashions ebbed and flowed, but, up to the Great Exhibition at least, it maintained a high degree of quality and craftsmanship. Although the method of applying black lacquer is usually called 'japanning' it bears little resemblance to the layers and layers of smooth resinous gum used by the Japanese for their lacquerware. The original Oriental technique had been anglicized as far back as the days of Queen Anne, when red 'English lacquer' bureaux, dressing-table mirrors and boxes first came into fashion. English lacquer on papier mâché is made with ten or twelve layers of shellac varnish, each coat 'stoved' or heated to harden it. Nineteenth-century English lacquerware is most commonly black, though during the

---

Chinese lacquer box and penwork handscreens
Height (box): 20.3 cm
Sold: Christie's, Great Tew Park, 28/5/87
Price: £660

'The Parlour', *tableau-mort* of stuffed squirrels
Height: 47.3 cm
Sold: Phillips, Oxford, 27/5/86
Price: £363

'Queen Anne' revival of the 1870s production of red lacquer increased, but the colour is either a dark maroon-red, or a near-scarlet which has usually faded. There was also a golden yellow, though this has often turned a muddy ochre as the varnish has darkened over the years. Dark green and dark blue were also used, but are far less common.

Inevitably, with their inability to know when to stop, the Victorians began to add small chips of mother-of-pearl to the decoration. It seemed such a good idea that soon the black lacquer surfaces were overloaded – simple flower decoration was highlighted, then smothered with gratuitous shell-inlay. Shells were imported from India and used in celebration of the elevation of Queen Victoria to 'Queen Empress' in the 1870s, and by the 1880s Australian supplies of dull-surfaced but slightly shimmering shells were plastered over cheap, pulpy versions of papier mâché.

A subtler form of decoration on lacquer was penwork, introduced during the Regency period and used mainly on chinoiserie furniture and decorative objects. Penwork is an extremely fine technique of hand-painting decoration on wood with a lacquer surface, with the details minutely finished in Indian ink with a quill pen. Originally the decoration was primarily in white on black lacquer, but from the 1830s on it was more often gilt on black.

Mahogany brass-bound writing slope
Height: 18.6 cm
McIntosh of Stockcross, Newbury
Price: £650

Japanned papier-mâché table
Width: 67.8 cm
Sold: Christie's, Orchardleigh Park, 21/9/87
Price: £550

NOVELTIES UNDER GLASS

By the last decades of the nineteenth century, every surface, every shelf of every family house, large or small, carried its cargo of souvenirs, gifts and handicrafts, from vases of cut paper flowers to marble mantel clocks, many of them heavy and oppressive, bearing the unmistakable stamp of the machine in their lack of finish and detail, and in the poor quality of their material and design. A thousand chimneys, industrial and domestic, filled the air with grime and soot, and defences of drapes and nets, chenilles and cretonnes, were erected to protect the furniture and furnishings against this frightening onslaught of dirt.

Because of the Victorians' morbid fascination for death, it is easy to suspect that glass domes were first manufactured in quantity to hold arrangements of artificial flowers as eternal symbols of potted grief, to stand in the shadow of every headstone and marble angel in the monu-

Scrapscreen
Height: 172.8 cm
Sold: Richard Breeze, London
Price: £475

mental cemeteries that were such a feature of Victorian England. Whether it was these ingenious bouquets of flowers that could withstand all weathers, or the arrival of the skeleton clock on mid-Victorian mantelpieces which prompted the adop-

tion of glass domes indoors, they neatly solved the problem of dust and dirt. Every decorative object went under glass – porcelain figures and groups from France and Italy, automata from Germany, flower arrangements in wool and wax for the front room and the parlour, stuffed birds fixed artistically to bits of bark for the bird watcher and nature lover, stuffed fish and sporting trophies for the hunter and the sportsman. Taxidermy flourished under these glass domes or in glass cases, and included tableaux of stuffed kittens, squirrels, mice and baby rabbits. They surely could not have been made for children, though the miniature furniture and the cosy, reassuringly domestic, anthropomorphic creatures might lead one to believe they were.

THE SCOTTISH LOVE AFFAIR

Sir Walter Scott began the English love-affair with Scotland in about 1820, with his novels and his house, Abbotsford, in Roxburghshire, in the 'Scottish baronial' style. But from 1854, when the Queen bought Balmoral and began to dress not only herself but also her children in plaids, shawls and kilts, Scottish fever assailed the English. People who barely knew the Lowlands from the Highlands added a pair of carvers with stag-horn handles to their sideboard cutlery drawers, self-consciously called their whisky 'drams' and drank it from thistle-shaped glasses, and fastened their tartan shawls with cloak-pins set with pieces of Cairngorm stone.

From the 1820s onwards there had been a steady trickle of visitors to the romantic heather-clad hills, and in Ayrshire and Kincardineshire craftsmen made card cases, snuff boxes and small souvenirs in fine-grained sycamore for the hardy travellers to take home. They were all made with beautifully fitting hinges which were an integral part of the box and the lid. In Mauchline and Cumnock in Ayrshire the boxes were often hand-painted with different-coloured wavy lines, rather like combed decoration. With the Victorian passion for plaid inevitably these wavy lines soon became tartan; in 1853 the firm of W. & A. Smith of Mauchline patented a multi-nibbed device for covering the boxes with plaid – generally that of the Royal Stuart, which was red and bright, or Hunting Stuart, which was dark green and black. In clan lore, these two plaids are the only ones permitted to be worn by the public at large – all others belong strictly to members of the clan alone.

Tartan ware increased in production for the tourist trade, with even cheaper methods of decoration. Printed tartan paper was glued to boxes and varnished, local views were transfer-printed, and the range was increased to encompass napkin rings, notebook covers, and even egg cups. Souvenirs from Laurencekirk in Kincardineshire consisted at first of snuff boxes with airtight lids and the integral 'Scottish hinges' in plain, well-finished sycamore or boxwood. From 1819 they were stamped with the name 'Stiven', a firm started in 1783 by Charles Stiven, which continued in production until 1868. Also made by W. & A. Smith were boxes which ingeniously imitated silver and niello inlay. The wooden carcases were covered in metal foil engraved with flowing patterns, painted and varnished. The results were much admired, and the company won a Gold Medal in 1851 for its products.   125

Object	Quality of manufacture	Quality of design and/or decoration	Rarity	Price (£)	Price ($)
Boxes					
brass casket inlaid with malachite	8	7	■ ■	500–800	950–1520
olivewood games box, brass-mounted	8	7	■ ■	400–700	760–1330
mother-of-pearl jewel box	8	6	■ ■ ■	250–500	475–950
gilt-bronze inkstand casket	7	6	■ ■ ■	700–1000	1330–1900
Russian lacquered box	8	6	■	150–550	285–1045
burr walnut liquor cabinet inlaid with mother-of-pearl	8	7	■ ■	200–400	380–760
walnut lap box	7	7	■ ■	400–700	760–1330
Clocks					
marble mantel clock	8	6	■	300–600	570–1140
glass-domed skeleton clock	7	7	■	350–650	665–1235
lighthouse clock	7	6	■ ■	500–800	950–1520
travelling timepiece	8	7	■ ■	600–1000+	1140–1900
gilt-metal strut timepiece	8	7	■ ■	500–800	950–1520
clock picture	7	7	■ ■	700–1000+	1330–1900+
Black Forest wall cuckoo clock	8	6	■ ■	400–800	760–1520
walnut or mahogany cased wall clock	7	7	■ ■	350–700	665–1330
mahogany longcase clock	7	6	■ ■	400–1000+	760–1900+
brass repeating carriage clock	7	7	■ ■	250–750	475–1425
bronzed spelter figural mystery timepiece	7	6	■ ■ ■	350–750	665–1425
Enamel					
Viennese scent flask	7	7	■ ■	200–400	380–760
Viennese silver-mounted cup and cover	7	7	■ ■ ■	700–1000+	1330–1900+
silver and enamel miniature birdcage	7	6	■ ■ ■	600–900	1140–1710

Qualities on a scale 1-10   ■ Rare   ■ ■ Very rare   ■ ■ ■ Extremely rare

Object	Quality of manufacture	Quality of design and/or decoration	Rarity	Price (£)	Price ($)
Ivory					
carved figural letter opener	7	7	■ ■	300–600	570–1140
figure	8	8	■ ■ ■	400–800	760–1520
goblet carved in relief with continuous hunting scene	8	6	■ ■ ■	600–1000+	1140–1900+
vierge ouvrante figure	8	7	■ ■ ■	400–1000+	760–1900+
Mauchline ware					
card case	7	6	■	40–100	75–190
snuff box	7	6	■	50–110	95–210
Miscellaneous					
tableau-mort of stuffed animals	8	4	■ ■ ■	250–500	475–950
Indian silvered filigree urn and cover	8	7	■ ■ ■	200–300	380–570
electrogilt candelabra centrepiece	7	7	■	600–800	1140–1520
gilt-bronze desk thermometer	8	7	■ ■ ■	700–1000	1330–1900
pair of gilt-bronze 'Empire' ewers	8	8	■ ■	750–1000	1425–1900
pair of cast-bronze 'Renaissance' ewers	7	8	■ ■	150–350	285–665
brass fender with pierced decoration	8	7	■ ■	500–800	950–1520
wheel barometer	8	6	■ ■	100–500	190–950
stick barometer	8	6	■ ■	250–750	475–1425
scrimshawed dolphin's jawbone	7	5	■ ■ ■	600–900	1140–1710
pair of scrimshawed whale's teeth	7	5	■ ■	350–700	665–1330

Qualities on a scale 1-10   ■ Rare   ■ ■ Very rare   ■ ■ ■ Extremely rare

Object	Quality of manufacture	Quality of design and/or decoration	Rarity	Price (£)	Price ($)
Papier mâché					
japanned table	7	7	■ ■	200–300	380–570
japanned and gilt chair	7	7	■	50–150	95–285
black and gilt japanned cigar box	7	7	■ ■	75–150	140–285
jewel cabinet inlaid with mother-of-pearl by Jennens & Bettridge	8	8	■ ■ ■	750–950	1425–1805
pair of face-screens by Jennens & Bettridge	8	7	■ ■ ■	350–550	665–1045
music stand inlaid with mother-of-pearl	7	6	■ ■	450–650	855–1235
pair of japanned and gilt spill vases	7	6	■ ■	250–450	475–855
Penwork					
hand screen	7	8	■ ■	75–150	140–285
jewel box	7	8	■ ■	300–600	570–1140
table cabinet	8	8	■ ■ ■	500–800	950–1520
Sculpture					
plaster reduction of Classical statue	7	8	■ ■	250–500	475–950
marble figure	7	7	■ ■	400–800	760–1520
bronze owl inkwell	7	7	■ ■ ■	450–850	855–1615
bronze figure of a bull (I. Bonheur)	8	8	■ ■ ■	700–1000	1330–1900
marble bust of a boy by Giovanni Bertoli	8	6	■ ■ ■	450–750	855–1425
marble bust of a girl (Italian)	8	7	■ ■ ■	500–1000+	950–1900+
pair of terracotta busts of young girls	8	6	■ ■ ■	600–900	1140–1710
bronze and ivory bust	7	5	■ ■	700–1000+	1330–1900+
patinated spelter figure	7	6	■	400–800	760–1520
Shellwork					
glass-domed group of shells	6	6	■ ■	150–300	285–570
picture	6	5	■	100–250	190–475

　Qualities on a scale 1-10　　■ Rare　　■ ■ Very rare　　■ ■ ■ Extremely rare

Object	Quality of manufacture	Quality of design and/or decoration	Rarity	Price (£)	Price ($)
Tortoiseshell					
tea caddy inlaid with ivory	8	7	■ ■	300–600	570–1140
inkstand inlaid with mother-of-pearl	8	7	■ ■	600–900	1140–1710
photograph frame	8	7	■ ■	250–500	475–950
Tunbridge ware					
rosewood tea caddy	8	6	■ ■ ■	300–600	570–1140
pencil box	6	6	■ ■	50–100	95–190

Qualities on a scale 1-10   ■ Rare   ■ ■ Very rare   ■ ■ ■ Extremely rare

CHAPTER SEVEN

TOYS
AND
GAMES

Box of picture bricks
Height: 9.7 cm
Hastwell & Howard, London
Price: £150

Carved and stained wood Noah's Ark
Length: 63.5 cm
Sold: Christie's, South Kensington, London, 2/10/86
Price: £352

Child may be so buried, that the new man may be raised up in him' and in the Catechism it stated that the child's duty is 'to keep my hands from picking and stealing, and my tongue from evil-speaking, lying and slandering'.

The rocking horse pursues the course
Directed by your hand,
Children should thus their friends obey
And do what they command.

When these moralizing lines were written in 1785, it was an astonishing fact that about a quarter of the population of England was under ten years old. From being disorderly nuisances, children had become a force to be reckoned with. The popular, and indeed religious, attitude that had prevailed up to this period had been that while a man was considered innocent until proved guilty in the eyes of the law, a child was not. At a christening, the invocation of blessing on the child included the prayer that 'the old Adam in this

Cast-iron clockwork hansom cab
Height: 28.7 cm
Sold: Christie's, South Kensington, London, 30/7/87
Price: £418

German doll's house furniture
Height (tallest piece): 20.3 cm
Sold: Phillips, London, 27/5/87
Price: £495

The shift in attitudes towards children can be seen in the child portraits painted by Gainsborough and Reynolds, and in a newer, more humane relationship within families. This was remarked upon by a French traveller, Henri Misson, who noted that 'They have an extraordinary Regard in *England* for young Chil-

dren, always flattering, always caressing, always applauding what they do; at least it seems so to us *French* folks, who correct our Children as soon as they are capable of reasoning, being of the Opinion, that to keep them in Awe is the best Way to give them a good Turn in their Youth.'

CHILDREN IN THEIR OWN RIGHT

Whatever the adult world thought of them, children had always played games, but seldom with toys. Games of tag, catch, French and English and Tom Tiddler's Ground had existed for

133

centuries, in one form or another. So had peg dolls, hoops, whips and tops, cup and ball, knucklebones and marbles, but not much else. There were musical boxes and wonderfully delicate automata, but these were toys for idle rich young ladies. With the remarkable change in attitude towards children, the first thirty years of the nineteenth century saw the beginnings of playthings made specifically to delight and amuse the small offspring which clustered around the skirts of their mothers.

Most toys of the first half of the century had a dual purpose: they were educational at the same time as being amusing. Boxes of building bricks doubled as simple jigsaw puz-

Model of a butcher's shop
Height: 16.8 cm
The Singing Tree, London
Price: £65

Toy dining-room dresser
Height: 25.3 cm
The Singing Tree, London
Price: £65

zles or alphabets, board games and card games taught geography or the dates of the Kings of England, rag books were no more than an extension of the old 'horn book' which taught reading and spelling. Boys were less catered for than girls – presumably because they were expected to learn the manly pursuits of horsemanship and sport. To this end, perhaps, the nursery rocking horse on curved rockers arrived at the end of the eighteenth century.

Dolls' houses belong to this early period, although they had existed for very privileged children centuries before. There were wooden pull-along toys, usually horses and traps, carved wooden dolls with jointed limbs, very basic rag dolls and, at the other end of the scale, precious, beautiful, richly dressed wax dolls. In these alone the English excelled:

'poured wax' dolls with mohair wigs, wax forearms and lower legs, and with exquisite wardrobes to conceal their cloth bodies, were even finer than imported French wax dolls. But oddly enough, though the English were plainly among the leaders in Europe of this new and enlightened attitude to children, British industry completely failed to gear itself up to making toys.

DOLLS' HOUSES

After 1815, free from the ravages of

Toy kitchen dresser in pine
Height: 22 cm
The Singing Tree, London
Price: £25

the Napoleonic Wars that had devastated their land, the gentle cult of Kirche, Küche und Kinder (church, kitchen and children) grew in Germany, Austria and Bavaria, and with it the beginnings of their toy industry. At first skilled wood carvers made 135

ing bricks, and most of the miniature furniture for every room in every Victorian nursery dolls' house. Many of the little wooden dolls, the families and the servants which lived in dolls' houses, came from the same source.

The English made rather grand dolls' houses in the Georgian style mostly opening at the back, while the French versions were more modest and were more likely to open at the front. In the mid-nineteenth century,

Oriental bisque doll by Simon & Halbig
Height: 48.6 cm
Sold: Sotheby's, Chester, 15/6/87
Price: £990

All-bisque boy doll
Height: 10.2 cm
The Singing Tree, London
Price: £95

the toys in softwood; they were finished and painted in small workshops in towns and villages and sold at fairs and markets. Toy-making was soon an organized, profitable affair, centred mainly around Nuremburg and Walterhausen; there, Noah's Arks were made, as well as boxed sets of farmyard animals and build-

many of the less expensive German
dolls' houses were made with printed
paper façades and miniature wall-
paper on the walls of the rooms. At
the very end of the century, the little
inhabitants were greatly improved by
porcelain heads. German and Bava-
rian toy-makers made painted
wooden miniature shops and market
stalls, but, for some reason, English
toy-makers seem to have made more
butchers' shops than anything else.

BABY DOLLS

With an eye on the broad middle-
class market, the Germans had
begun to make dolls' heads and
shoulders in one piece, using a base
similar to plaster of Paris, with wax
modelling over it and tresses of natural hair, though the bodies were still
made of stuffed cloth. From the
1840s some 'shoulder-headed' dolls
were made in papier mâché, mainly
in Germany, as well as some early
'wind-up' dolls with clockwork movements from France. But papier
mâché was not very durable, and was
soon replaced with 'bisque', around
the 1860s. More expensive dolls had
been made with porcelain heads, but
'bisque', a once-fired, matt-finish
porcelain, was far more realistic and
less expensive to make.

Up to this time, dolls were, in the
main, miniature adults, and the most
precious were those which came with
more than a simple shift, to be
dressed by nannies and nursery-
maids. German dolls in particular
were often beautifully dressed, and
the more expensive ones often came
with a wardrobe of beautifully made
dresses and petticoats. But with the
general movement towards more
naturalistic forms, doll manufacturers concentrated on more lifelike

All-bisque girl doll
Height: 9.3 cm
The Singing Tree, London
Price: £75

'baby' dolls with chubby, jointed
limbs and baby faces. At first, only
the arms were made with a ball-and-
socket joint, then arms and wrists,
and finally the whole body, tinted an
orange-pink flesh colour, was made
with movable, jointed arms and legs
and swivel necks.

Germany and France were running
neck and neck in the race for the
baby-doll market. In the 1870s Germany began to produce all-bisque
dolls in huge quantities and a wide

137

variety of models, some with moulded head and hair and jointless bodies, some jointed with wigs. Best-known makers of early all-bisque dolls were Silbur & Fleming, Strasburger and Pfeiflen & Co. and they were very cheap indeed, so cheap that they could be bought in the corner candy store or sweet shop on both sides of the Atlantic.

The possibilities of combining bisque heads with composition bodies were exploited, and Léon Casimir Bru and his son made Bru bébé dolls with soft kid bodies, bisque swivel heads on bisque shoulders, with bisque forearms and

> **Costume dolls by S.F.B.J.**
> Height: 12.5 cm
> The Singing Tree, London
> Price (each): £75

hands and wood-and-compo legs. But without a doubt the most successful and the most famous of all doll-makers in the last decade of the nineteenth century was Armand Marseille, a cunning German manu-facturer whose name was intended to convince buyers that the product was French. Armand Marseille gave the

French doll-making industry such a fright that all the companies combined to form the Société Française de Bébés et Jouets (S.F.B.J.) in order to compete.

BOOKS

Queen Victoria's happy brood of children undoubtedly had a great effect on English families, as well as the gentle, paternal behaviour of Prince Albert, who happily played 'bears' with his children – a thing no stiff Englishman would have contemplated. By the late 1850s and 1860s though, the tolerance of parents appears to have run out, and there was a new, harsher spirit abroad. Victorian children were to be seen and not heard. Children had never been allowed to play games on Sundays – a tradition which lingered long after the Victorian era had passed in many strict homes. But along with the new morality and stiff starchiness that characterized the mid-nineteenth century, their innocence was no longer presumed. The Book of Proverbs was scanned for such *bons mots* as 'He that spareth his rod hateth his son', and 'Train up a child in the way he should go: and when he is old, he will not depart from it.'

The growing number of children's books were preoccupied with sinful children, dying children, wicked children who got their just desserts, and, of course, Little Lord Fauntleroy, the goodiest goody-goody of all time. Mercifully the printing industry came to the rescue, and Deans, Routledge and Frederick Warne began to produce an entirely new and totally sympathetic kind of book. Kate Greenaway, Walter Crane and Randolph Caldecott were all printed by the thousand in the 1870s and had a lasting, delightful influence on their young readers' lives.

WIND-UP TOYS AND TIN SOLDIERS

By the middle of the nineteenth century, French clockmakers had turned the making of clocks of all sizes into a major industry, and were pre-eminent in the manufacture of automata. Around the 1860s they began making simple clockwork toys but were challenged by the Germans who began to make tinplate 'wind-ups' at about the same time. In Germany and France the race was on to mass produce dolls and toys of all kinds. There were pull-along toys in cast iron, wood and papier mâché, which

China-headed doll
Height: 12 cm
The Singing Tree, London
Price: £75

performed simple movements as the wheels went round. Wind-up toys with enamel or transfer-printed bodies, from performing dogs and clowns to jaw-snapping lions and tigers, came from the tinplate-makers of Germany and France, and those from the Fernand Martin factory were particularly ingenious. German Noah's Arks from the 1860s and 1870s had dozens of pairs of animals, the wood highly polished, and by the 1870s the first 'tin soldiers' made in Germany in flat die-cast metal were being marshalled in platoons on nursery floors. Soon after, superior, English hollow-cast battalions with bright enamelled regimental colours attacked and ad-

vanced across the carpet.

By the last decades of the century, the American toy industry was geared up to make mainly mechanical, tinplate and wind-up toys of a totally different character from Europe. Among the first successful lines were mechanical moneyboxes, toy banks and shops, followed by mules and donkeys, circus animals and clockwork merry-go-rounds and carousels. The Germans, quick to open up new markets, began to make dolls' house furniture in designs by Duncan Phyfe and dolls' houses in Colonial style. By this time the German factories were also supplying a feast of miniature tableware complete with fish on dishes, joints of beef and puddings made in china, as well as little dolls' house dolls.

TINPLATE TRAINS AND LIMOUSINES

If the middle decades of the nineteenth century belonged to little

---

Locomotive by Stevens
Height: 15.4 cm
Sold: Christie's, South Kensington,
London, 30/7/87
Price: £605

girls, the 1880s and 1890s belonged to the boys. Steam trains rattled across the countryside, and after the initial excitement put all England into a high degree of Railway Fever, the Great Western, the London and North Eastern and the London, Midland and Scottish joint stock railway companies were floated, and trains became part of life. So, too, did motor cars, but in many ways they lacked the panting excitement of the great trains with their carriages in the smart liveries of their companies. The British were, however, unable to capitalize on the manufacture of tinplate trains, and once again it was a German tinplate toy-maker which captured the market. Marklin, which had been making tinplate toys since the 1860s, began making model locomotives, tracks and signal systems which were copied by many small firms making mechanical tinplate toys. Marklin trains, tenders and carriages were made with the correct liveries of the railway companies, and GWR, LNER and LMS locomotives are among the most beautifully made and finished toys ever produced.

Other German companies also

Wooden model of a brewers' dray
Length: 67.8 cm
Sold: Christie's, Orchardleigh Park, 22/9/87
Price: £176

capitalized on clockwork toys, among them Carette, Lehmann, Gunthermann and Bing. Gebrüder Bing today is probably better known for its limousines and motor cars than its trains, although the English firm of Bassett-Lowke bought Carette, Bing and Marklin locomotives which they marketed under their own name. Clockwork limousines, although beautifully detailed, enamelled and finished, are not immediately identifiable as models of early motor cars, and it was not until the twentieth century that recognizable Mercedes, Citroëns and Fords were made. Right at the very end of the nineteenth century, American toy manufacturers entered the race – and for American boys it was the glamour of the open road and the automobile which had the most appeal, far more than the railway track.

Object	Quality of manufacture	Quality of design and/or decoration	Rarity	Price (£)	Price ($)
Cast iron					
clockwork hansom cab and horse	6	7	■	350–550	665–1045
J. & E. Stevens mechanical money box	6	6	■	150–350	285–665
William Tell mechanical bank (American)	7	7	■ ■	300–500	570–950
'Lion and Monkeys' money box by Kyser & Rex	7	7	■ ■	200–400	380–760
Dolls					
French bisque shoulder-headed	7	7	■	300–1000+	570–1900+
German bisque-headed	7	7	■	250–1000+	475–1900+
Franz Schmidt bisque-headed	7	7	■ ■	700–1000+	1330–1900+
Simon & Halbig Oriental bisque	8	7	■ ■ ■	750–1000	1425–1900
Pierotti wax shoulder-headed	7	6	■ ■	400–800	760–1520
Charles Marsh wax shoulder-headed	7	6	■ ■	350–550	665–1045
Jules Steiner Bourgoin bisque-headed	7	6	■ ■ ■	700–1000+	1330–1900+
Heubach china-headed doll	7	7	■	120–240	230–455
Bahr & Proschild bisque-headed	7	7	■	250–500	475–950
Armand Marseille bisque-headed 'Dollie'	7	6	■	200–400	380–760
Armand Marseille bisque-headed character	7	7	■ ■	500–1000+	950–1900+
Armand Marseille china-headed small	6	7	■	60–120	115–230
Armand Marseille Oriental bisque-headed baby	6	6	■ ■	350–550	665–1045
S.F.B.J. small costume	6	7	■ ■	75–150	140–285
S.F.B.J. bisque-headed character	7	7	■ ■ ■	700–1000+	1330–1900+

Qualities on a scale 1-10   ■ Rare   ■ ■ Very rare   ■ ■ ■ Extremely rare

Object	Quality of manufacture	Quality of design and/or decoration	Rarity	Price (£)	Price ($)
Dolls' house furniture					
suite of dining-room furniture	7	6	■ ■	350–550	665–1045
kitchen dresser	6	6	■ ■	20–80	40–150
dining-room dresser	6	7	■ ■	40–100	75–190
French miniature open kitchen	8	6	■ ■ ■	350–550	665–1045
rattan and leather three-piece suite	7	7	■ ■	250–500	475–950
miniature grandfather clock	7	6	■ ■	150–300	285–570
Lead figures					
Britain's Bombay Lancers (original box)	7	7	■ ■	400–600	760–1140
Britain's Flying Trapeze (original box)	7	6	■ ■ ■	900–1000+	1710–1900+
Britain's Royal Horse Artillery (1st version)	7	7	■ ■	700–900	1330–1710
Britain's Scots Guards (original box)	7	6	■ ■	200–400	380–760
24-piece elephant-hunting set	6	6	■ ■ ■	350–550	665–1045
Britain's horse-drawn 18 in. heavy howitzer (original box)	7	7	■ ■ ■	800–1000	1520–1900
Imperial Russian Guard, 68 pieces, German	6	6	■ ■ ■	300–450	570–855
Cossack cavalry, 25 pieces, probably German	7	7	■ ■ ■	600–800	1140–1520
Games					
mahogany shove ha'penny board	7	6	■ ■ ■	60–120	115–230
bagatelle	7	5	■ ■	25–50	50–95
leather-boxed bézique with ivory markers	8	6	■ ■ ■	150–250	285–475

Qualities on a scale 1-10   ■ Rare   ■ ■ Very rare   ■ ■ ■ Extremely rare   143

Object	Quality of manufacture	Quality of design and/or decoration	Rarity	Price (£)	Price ($)
Mechanical toys					
clockwork old woman	7	6	■ ■	200–400	380–760
'L'Hercule Populaire' strong man	7	6	■ ■ ■	350–500	665–950
'General Butler' walking figure by Ives	7	6	■ ■ ■	900–1000+	1710–1900+
clockwork dancing bear	7	6	■ ■	250–500	475–950
clockwork performing seal	7	6	■ ■	300–600	570–1140
Tinplate					
Vielmetter wind-up toy	7	7	■ ■	500–1000+	950–1900+
Bing fish	6	6	■ ■	200–400	380–760
Carette sailboat	6	6	■ ■	200–400	380–760
French nodding tiger	7	6	■ ■	300–600	570–1140
Bing three-funnel liner	7	7	■ ■ ■	500–900	950–1710
Lehmann beetle	6	5	■ ■	100–300	190–570
clown musician	7	6	■ ■	200–500	380–950
bagatelle player	7	5	■ ■	200–300	380–570
carousel	7	6	■ ■	150–250	285–475
Bing gunboat	7	7	■ ■ ■	600–800	1140–1520

Qualities on a scale 1-10   ■ Rare   ■ ■ Very rare   ■ ■ ■ Extremely rare

Object	Quality of manufacture	Quality of design and/or decoration	Rarity	Price (£)	Price ($)
Trains					
Marklin 'Power Car'	7	6	■ ■	400–600	760–1140
Bing baggage car	7	6	■	200–300	380–570
Stevens brass locomotive	8	8	■ ■	500–700	950–1330
H. J. Wood brass and steel locomotive and tender	8	8	■ ■	650–850	1235–1615
Carette L.N.W.R. passenger coach	7	6	■	200–400	380–760
Marklin gauge 'I' locomotive	7	7	■ ■	100–200	190–380
Merkelbach metal and brass steam locomotive	8	7	■ ■ ■	750–1000	1425–1900
Bing spirit-fired gauge 'II' locomotive	7	7	■ ■	150–400	285–760
Rock & Graner gauge 'O' station	7	7	■ ■ ■	500–800	950–1520
Marklin painted tin warehouse	7	7	■ ■ ■	600–900	1140–1710
Wood					
box of picture bricks	6	7	■ ■	100–300	190–570
boxed set of animals	7	6	■ ■	250–500	475–950
carved and stained wood Noah's Ark and animals	7	7	■ ■	250–750	475–1425
pair of carved and stained wood wind-up dancers	6	6	■ ■	250–500	475–950
pull-along brewer's dray	7	7	■ ■	150–250	285–475
seesaw	7	5	■ ■ ■	300–500	570–950
carved and stained wood rocking horse	7	7	■ ■	600–1000+	1140–1900+

Qualities on a scale 1-10   ■ Rare   ■ ■ Very rare   ■ ■ ■ Extremely rare   145

CHAPTER   EIGHT

JEWELLERY

Gold and garnet locket brooch
Height: 13.5 cm
Sold: Christie's, South Kensington,
London, 6/10/87
Price: £770

The Victorian era marked the end of the long dominance of the male as peacock, and his swift transference from wearing a fortune to investing a fortune in gems and jewellery which were worn by women. 'There she is, with poor Eustace's twenty thousand pounds round her neck', said Laurence Fitzgibbon to his friend Barrington Earle in Anthony Trollope's *The Eustace Diamonds*, published in 1873. Until the Married Women's Property Act of 1870, all money and property was vested in the man of the house, and if he could not wear his fortune himself, he wanted his wife and daughters to show it off – in diamonds, preferably, or in the largest stones he could afford or had inherited. The Married Women's Property Act graciously allowed women to keep as their own the money that they had earned by their own work.

Diamond brooch
Height: 5.2 cm
Sold: Bonham's, London, 27/11/87
Price: £715

ELEGANCE AND PROPRIETY

In the early years of Victoria's reign a young lady of fashion and good family

Gold bracelet with pierced decoration
Length: 18 cm
Sold: Bonham's, London, 30/10/87
Price: £682

wore little in the way of jewellery, and an unmarried one never wore diamonds, though there were always flighty exceptions. Her jewellery was usually handed down to her and consisted of a gold chain from which hung a small gold watch, a locket or a crucifix, a string of well-matched pearls, a few pairs of earrings, and a sprinkling of jewelled pins for her hair, when she became old enough to 'put it up' to show she was no longer a child.

Compared with the totally immodest appearance of the late Regency period, when a young woman's dress was a mere scrap of clinging, diaphanous material revealing bare neck and shoulders, and her hair was piled with extravagant ornament, a young woman in the early years of the Victorian era was likely to be a picture of modesty. Jewelled combs held ringlets and curls, circlets of gold and pearls were threaded through her hair, or a thin band, set low on her forehead in the classical Greek style, was decorated with jewelled flowers or sunburst sprays. Strings of pearls were looped and plaited into the hair itself, now drawn smoothly over the head. Young, newly married women might also sprinkle pretty little diamond stars in their hair or on their bodices. These little stars were all the rage in the previous century when Halley's comet streaked through the sky and sparked off a new interest in astronomy. Stars and sunbursts were often part of a larger piece of jewellery which could be detached and worn separately, sparkling yet demure. But by day, a locket, gold chain and a few bracelets, often with little Wedgwood cameo plaques or perhaps with Apsley Pellatt's cameo sulphides, with brooches and earrings to match, were considered to be adornment enough.

Hardstone cameo earrings with diamonds and pearls
Height: 4.2 cm
Sold: Bonham's, London, 27/11/87
Price: £748

NATURAL, ROMANTIC AND RESTRAINED

In 1840 Queen Victoria married Prince Albert and was free to adorn herself more grandly. Fashions changed radically, with waists drawn in above full, billowing skirts, low necklines, shoulder knots, lace and ribbons. At last there were new opportunities for wearing the family diamonds, reset in the new fashion,

Gold-mounted carved agate cameo brooch
Height: 4 cm
Sold: Bonham's, London, 27/11/87
Price: £396

MEDIEVAL SPLENDOUR

The bare-shouldered beauties of the 1840s admired the far more vigorous and colourful jewellery of France, Italy and Austria in neo-Renaissance designs, a style originated by Fortunato Pio Castellani of Rome. Almost all of this beautiful work was taken straight from sixteenth-century miniatures and court portraits, and suited the prevailing romantic passion for themes from the Middle Ages. Amethysts, aquamarines, peridots, garnets, citrines and pale topaz were set in tiny panels of enamel and linked with rows of pearls, the stones foiled at the back to enhance the brilliance of colour and depth. Castellani greatly influenced other designers such as Giacinto Mellilo of Naples, Eugène often incorporating large rose-cut stones which had previously been worn on the coats and waistcoats of gentlemen.

In France and Italy there was a revival of lush rococo styles, but the English were ill at ease with *la volupté* and in their hands the sensuous, scrolling, naturalistic shapes were safely domesticated. Classical serpents became common or garden snakes and lizards; instead of lush, stylized, gem-set flowers there were sprays of turquoise forget-me-nots and seed-pearl daisies; and barbaric bangles shrank to ladylike bracelets. The Queen herself set one of the most enduring fashions around this time – the strap-and-buckle bracelet, based on the Order of the Garter, the regalia of which she, as sovereign, was entitled to wear.

Shell cameo earring
Height: 3.1 cm
Sold: Bonham's, London, 18/9/87
Price (pair): £385

Necklace of foiled garnets
Length: 55.5 cm
Sold: Bonham's, London, 30/10/87
Price: £605

Fontenay of France and Robert Phillips and the Giuliano family in London, who all made similar, remarkably fine neo-Renaissance jewellery in the first half of the nineteenth century.

There was a distinct and telling dislike of 'paste' – to the thoroughbred English it meant vulgar and shallow, and condemned the character of the wearer. 'Lady Eustace was a woman of whom it might be almost said that she ought to wear diamonds ... the only doubt might be whether paste might not better suit her character. But these were not paste, and she did shine and glitter and was very rich.'

In America, however, where jewellery was rare and precious gems were seldom worn at this period, Charles Louis Tiffany opened his business in New York in 1839 with a shipment of German paste jewellery which was snapped up so quickly and with such profit that it proved to be the foundation for Tiffany's empire of luxury and good taste. By 1844, when a 30 per cent tariff was imposed on all imported goods, Tiffany could afford to drop his inexpensive but pretty lines, and he started to import the very best gems and jewellery from Paris, London and Rome. In 1848 he began to make his own jewellery.

CAMEOS, SOUVENIRS AND ARCHAEOLOGICAL THEMES

The good taste and obvious provenance of Italian-made jewellery were infinitely preferable to cheap copies of more traditional pieces. Fashionable honeymoon couples, scholars and aristocrats had all made their pilgrimages to the cradle of the Renaissance from the eighteenth century onwards, bringing back souvenirs of fine Italian jewellery. In 1856 Thomas Cook inaugurated his travel service, which linked railways to steamers and opened up the hitherto privileged 'Grand Tour' to anyone who could afford his modest prices. The jewellers and trinket-makers of Florence, Rome and Naples were quick to adapt to the new tourism, making a range of inexpensive 'souvenir' jewellery for an increasing number of culture-hungry visitors.

Cameo heads were nothing new, but until the mid-nineteenth century they had been expensively made from hardstone and gemstone. They had been fashionable in England and

151

Gold bracelet with Wedgwood jasperware plaques
Length: 17.8 cm
Sold: Bonham's, London, 18/9/87
Price: £550

France from the end of the eighteenth century when many fashions were inspired by the extensive excavations of Pompeii and Herculaneum. By the mid-nineteenth century Italy and France were producing curiosities such as medallions set as bracelets, brooches and rings made of Pompeiian lava, with classical heads in white or a number of suitably earthy colours. Striated agate was cut and polished, or the striations used to great effect in low relief. Cameos were made of shells instead of stones, and there was hardly a household of any standing in Europe which did not possess a piece of Italian mosaic work. Made from minute chips of coloured stone, with quite remarkable craftsmanship, brooches, medallions, earrings and necklaces bore tiny views of Roman ruins, birds, flowers, classical horseheads, vine leaves and a score of other good, mediocre and poor designs. They were all mounted in thin gold settings and were sold in their hundreds.

The revived arts of cloisonné and champlevé enamelling are much in evidence in the very fine 'archaeological' jewellery of the 1850s. It is a confusing period, with several quite distinct influences overlapping each other. At about the same time, Queen Victoria fell in love with Scotland (she bought Balmoral in 1854) and Scottish pebble jewellery seized the public imagination. Bold, barbaric Celtic designs also became highly fashionable after the mid-century, partly because a great deal of Irish and Scottish work was shown at the Great Exhibition.

Gold and enamel brooch
Height: 3.4 cm
Sold: Boham's, London, 30/10/87
Price: £110

COMMONPLACE GOLD AND PASTICHE

Other, more pedestrian influences were to have a far more telling effect on jewellery in the mid-Victorian period than artistic design and inspiration had. Paste was not the only imitator of great wealth; there was pinchbeck too, a substitute for gold invented in the eighteenth century. And in 1817 a technique for working gold economically, which was similar to silver 'Sheffield plate', joined the cheaper jeweller's stock in trade. Known as 'rolled gold', it consisted of two thin layers of gold fused to base metal, and was used for bracelets, mounts and plain, heavy settings. After 1840, electro-gilding made 'cheapjack jewellery' a commonplace in every fairground and market.

Gold was no longer the rare and precious metal it had once been. In 1849, miners struck gold in California and precipitated 'The Gold Rush'. Ten years later it was being mined in Colorado, Australia, and many other parts of the accessible world. In 1854 in England, the Goldsmith's Company permitted three lower standards to be brought into use: in addition to 22 carat and 18 carat, gold could be made in 15 carat, 12 carat and 9 carat, doubtless to encourage the new bourgeoisie to buy the genuine metal and not mere tinsel counterfeit. From the 1860s

Diamond, ruby and gold scrollwork brooch
Height: 12.8 cm
Sold: Christie's, South Kensington, London, 18/2/86
Price: £750

onwards, jewellery design becomes so confusingly repetitive that the quality of the gold is often a more reliable guide to dating and hence value. The most favoured standard for good-quality, less expensive jewellery throughout the nineteenth century was 15 carat (though small pieces are not usually hallmarked), and if tests show a piece to be mere 9 carat, this indicates that it was of poor quality even when made, and better can be found. Moreover, 9 carat is still in general use today, so a 9-carat piece may be a recent reproduction, whereas 12-carat and 15-carat have been discontinued.

BLOOD RED AND CORAL PINK

Garnets and gold were an extremely popular combination for the more traditional jewellery in the middle years of the century: great blood-red carbuncles encircled with seed pearls were set deep into 'bloomed gold' with a matt finish; lesser pieces had small garnets set as eyes for snakes, dragonflies and lizards, or as flowerheads in sprays. Amethysts were also highly regarded, and had always been classified as gemstones; their deep, rich purple-red had been associated for centuries with the jewelled copes and mitres of the clergy, and it was not until later in the century, when amethyst was

> **Micro-mosaic brooch**
> Height: 3.4 cm
> Sold: Bonham's, London, 27/11/87
> Price: £506

found to be no more than a coloured quartz, that it fell from grace. Topaz from Brazil, as dark as a good rich sherry, was much prized from about 1780 onwards and was often used in association with pearls. Heated, the sherry-coloured stone turns a delicate rose-pink, which was considered appropriate for young girls' jewellery.

Also among the lively, colourful jewellery of the 1850s and 1860s was coral, imported in its raw state from Naples, where it was mainly confined to necklaces and pendants for very small children, since it was believed to ward off the evil eye. But in the hands of jewellers inspired by Castellani's Etruscan work, coral was carved, polished and set in gold, for cloak-clasps, earrings and pendants like classical disc-shaped shields, or made into long, dangling earrings. Coral was carved for cameos and in conjunction with fine enamelled work, or with fine gold mesh for necklaces and bracelets, particularly after Castellani's work was seen at the International Exhibition of 1862 in London.

MOURNING JEWELLERY

In 1861 Prince Albert died, plunging a nation and a great deal of its Empire into deepest mourning. Sentimental mourning jewellery, made from the hair of the dear departed, had been a maudlin fashion in the last decades of the eighteenth century, and had always been part of women's repertoire of daytime jewellery.

With the Queen herself taking the lead, personal adornment suffered an almost total eclipse for a number of years, with the exception of colourless stones and jet. The last was in

Turquoise and diamond stockpin
Length: 9.2 cm
Sold: Bonham's, London, 30/10/87
Price: £110

such demand that for a brief time jet from the cliffs of Whitby, on the bleak north-eastern coast of England, was more in demand than diamonds from Kimberley (discovered in South Africa in the same year as Albert's death). In fact, jet jewellery had been briefly in fashion in Britain after the death of William IV in 1837; it particularly became popular in France, where it was used to highlight black velvet and lace in the early 1850s.

Mourning jewellery was also made 155

from black onyx, black enamel and, quite difficult to distinguish from jet, black glass. Known as 'French jet', it is heavier than the light, fossilized black driftwood of Whitby, and surprisingly lacks the soft but brilliant shine that is so characteristic of well-polished jet jewellery. The Spanish, too, made their own variety of jet, but by the 1880s, though Queen Victoria remained in mourning, the fashion had burnt itself out and jet jewellery was not revived until during the 1920s.

OPALS AND MOONSTONES

The colourless or nearly colourless stones that were permitted for ladies in full mourning included white topaz, opals and pale fiery moonstones. These mysterious stones changed colour and, according to some, acted as a barometer of the wearer's mood. There may be a grain

of truth in the myth, since opals are affected by moisture, and the condition of a lady's skin might well indicate her nervousness or confidence. The incredible Hungarian Opal, nearly 5 cm (2 in) long, was one of the opulent stones on exhibition at the Crystal Palace, and attracted almost as much attention as the spectacular Koh-i-Noor Diamond and the lavishly jewelled sword-hilts and ceremonial daggers of the Ottoman Empire and the Moghuls of India.

The Indian Mutiny broke out in 1857 and, inspired by the many legends and the notorious ferocity of some Indian sects as seen to be manifested in the Bengal uprising against British rule, Wilkie Collins wrote *The Moonstone*, published in 1863. The plot centres around a fabulous stone looted at Seringapatam, and pinpoints accurately the contemporary fascination for these strange, unearthly gems. It was the iridescent opal, however, that had gained the reputation of being unlucky, and not the moonstone. The belief is more likely to have been generated by the fact that opals expand and contract, and if this property is not taken into account by the jeweller, the stones may fall out of their settings.

Child & Child enamel and cultured pearl brooch
Height: 3.7 cm
Sold: Christie's, South Kensington, London, 6/10/87
Price: £264

Turquoise and diamond earrings
Height: 6.5 cm
Sold: Bonham's, London, 27/11/87
Price: £825

JAPANESE LACQUER AND BUTTERFLY WINGS

As time passed after Prince Albert's death, the Court was permitted to wear half-mourning, and stones with purple, lilac or lavender colouring were permitted. But already the Aesthetes had begun to promote an entirely new vogue, and across the Atlantic, Japanese influence had become a major factor in jewellery design. In the 1860s French merchants introduced small lacquerwork, ivories and textiles to Paris, and by the 1870s the entire Western world had found a new impetus for its flagging repertoire of design. The Aesthetic Movement had already revived the delicate art of tortoiseshell piqué, an ancient craft from Naples dating back to the sixteenth century. This was a cunning method of fixing patterns of pinpricks of gold or silver in tortoiseshell by the simple expedient of expansion and contraction. The pattern was pricked into the heated shell, pinpricks of precious metal inserted and, when the shell cooled, remained locked into its pattern. Pursuing naturalism in raw materials as well as form, the Aesthetes had also begun the fashion for long strings of amber beads.

Japonaiserie fitted well with the Aesthetes' scheme of things – black lacquer and gold, beautifully carved tiny ivories and the shimmering rainbow colours of Japanese silks were perfectly in tune with their lofty ideals. In the hands of master-craftsmen, all these new effects were exploited admirably, with the exception of the 'shot silk' shimmer, which led to a long line of poor imitations. Butterflies' wings were set under glass and surrounded with filigree work for brooches, necklaces and earrings, or mounted realistically in the long trail of dragonfly, beetle and 'novelty' jewellery.

INDIAN FILIGREE AND SERMONS IN STONES

Popular taste was far more patriotic and conservative than that of the Aesthetes. In the 1870s, when Queen Victoria became Empress of India, 157

there was a craze for turquoise. The British believed that these brightly coloured, relatively inexpensive stones came from India, though in fact they came mainly from Persia. Indian brooches and silver filigree jewellery were also popular, and imported by the crate.

Lockets, never out of fashion, were no longer handmade or individually commissioned, but mass produced with steel dies which were able to stamp out both sides of a locket, including hinge and clasp, in a single operation. The human touch was added by flowers, hearts or stars, in coloured stones which spelled out 'Dearest' or 'Regard'. The latter were particularly popular and brooches and pins bearing the word were made

> **Gold filigree and coral earrings**
> Height: 7.6 cm
> Sold: Bonham's, London, 18/12/87
> Price: £770

by the hundred.

Garnets, briefly out of fashion, returned; they were no longer cabochons, but rose-cut in clusters of flowerheads on necklaces, brooches and earrings. The work of a second generation of Giulianos came into fashion; though often referred to as 'Holbein' jewellery, it was actually derived not from Holbein's paintings but from portraits by Quentin Matsys, a Dutch painter of the same period.

DIAMONDS AND PEARLS

In 1884 miners struck gold in the Transvaal, and Australia was yielding gold and precious gems in inordinate amounts. But it was the 'Big Hole' of Kimberley, 1.6 km (1 mile) around the top and 213 m (almost 700 ft) deep, enmeshed with the ropes and pendant buckets of anything up to 50,000 men digging for diamonds, that so emphatically influenced the last two decades of the nineteenth century.

The Astors, the Rockefellers, the Vanderbilts, the Woolworths and the Rothschilds wore diamonds all day, every day, as a matter of course. There were some English ladies, though, who almost went one better. Lady Carew, for example, had her portrait painted in 1886, in which her dress was loaded with ten great diamond brooches round its low neckline, not one of them remotely related in shape, style or design. French and American women sported sautoires — neck chains as long as skipping ropes, set with diamonds. Tiers of pearls supported swan-like necks; they were perfectly matched and perfectly round, with as many as twelve strands strung between thin discs of silver to keep them separate. There were ropes of wonderful pearls, too, as well as chokers, and bibs which spread over neck and collarbone in colours which graduated from pinks through every shade of cream to pearl grey.

In the 1890s Carl Fabergé was ringing the changes on diamond-studded enamels, and added diamond-encrusted flower-baskets, initials and monograms to the catalogue of opulence. Little Fabergé animals were imitated on pins and brooches, swelling the whole fantas-tic menagerie of every jeweller's shop and department store. In the last few years of the Victorian era, gold settings were heavy and gems were scattered with abandon over every surface, but hand in hand with this extravagance went paste and silver, tawdry gilt and tiny chips of anonymous stone or even glass. It had to look opulent, whatever the materials used.

Rose diamond rivière necklace
Length: 57.3 cm
Sold: Bonham's, London, 30/10/87
Price: £715

Object	Quality of manufacture	Quality of design and/or decoration	Rarity	Price (£)	Price ($)
Bracelets					
ruby and diamond cluster	7	7	■ ■	450–650	855–1235
gold star work	8	7	■ ■	500–700	950–1330
gold-mounted Wedgwood jasperware	8	8	■ ■ ■	400–600	760–1140
garnet, gold and diamond	7	7	■ ■	400–600	760–1140
serpent-headed gold, ruby, diamond and enamel	8	8	■ ■	800–1000+	1520–1900+
silver-mounted Scotch pebble	7	7	■ ■	50–100	95–190
Brooches					
antique carved agate cameo and gold	8	6	■	250–400	475–760
micro-mosaic	8	6	■ ■	350–600	665–1140
cushion-cut diamond star	8	6	■	500–750	950–1425
gold and enamel	7	7	■ ■	75–150	140–285
gold, enamel and diamond	8	7	■ ■	300–450	570–855
gold and diamond	8	7	■ ■	400–600	760–1140
chrysoberyl, foiled pink topaz and gold	7	7	■ ■ ■	500–700	950–1330
diamond, ruby and gold scrollwork	8	7	■ ■	600–800	1140–1520
enamel 'wing' set with pearls	7	6	■	200–300	380–570
carbuncle and gold locket	8	6	■ ■	600–800	1140–1520
'Etruscan'-style enamel and gold locket	8	7	■ ■ ■	900–1000+	1710–1900+
pearl	7	7	■	100–200	190–380
shell cameo	7	6	■	400–700	760–1330
gold, diamond and onyx cameo	8	7	■ ■	500–800	950–1520
ruby and pearl lizard	7	6	■ ■	250–400	475–760
gold and green hardstone vine	8	6	■ ■ ■	150–300	285–570

Qualities on a scale 1-10   ■ Rare   ■ ■ Very rare   ■ ■ ■ Extremely rare

Object	Quality of manufacture	Quality of design and/or decoration	Rarity	Price (£)	Price ($)
Earrings					
hardstone cameo, diamond and pearls	7	7	■ ■	600–800	1140–1520
diamond and turquoise	8	8	■ ■ ■	600–800	1140–1520
filigree gold and coral	8	8	■ ■ ■	600–800	1140–1520
shell cameo	7	6	■	250–500	475–950
banded agate and diamond	7	6	■ ■	150–300	285–570
gold, opal, seed pearl and enamel	7	7	■ ■	300–400	570–760
gold, enamel and pearl	8	8	■ ■	450–750	855–1425
carved Whitby jet	7	6	■ ■	50–100	95–190
amethyst and diamond	7	7	■ ■	400–600	760–1140
Necklaces					
micro-mosaic	8	6	■ ■	700–900	1330–1710
foiled garnet	8	7	■ ■	400–600	760–1140
gold and carbuncle	7	7	■	800–1000+	1520–1900+
red amber	7	6	■ ■	150–300	285–570
gold and split seed pearl	8	6	■	500–700	950–1330
Pendants					
gold-mounted garnet cross	8	6	■ ■	200–400	380–760
Stockpins					
turquoise and diamond	7	7	■ ■	75–150	140–285
ruby, diamond and pearl	7	7	■ ■	50–100	95–190
ruby and white enamel	7	6	■ ■	100–200	190–380
diamond and pearl	7	6	■ ■	75–150	140–285

Qualities on a scale 1-10   ■ Rare   ■ ■ Very rare   ■ ■ ■ Extremely rare

INDEX

Pages in italics contain
illustrations

A

acid-etching 103
Adams Bros. 84, 121
Aesthetes, The 15, *16*
Aesthetic movement *16*, 17
  furniture *34*
  glass 105
  jewellery 157
Albert, Prince Consort 10,
  11, 12
  death 31, 155, 157
Albert Memorial (engraving)
  12
Allerton, Charles, & Sons 71
aluminium 83
amber 157
'Amberina' glass 106
America *see* USA
American Porcelain factory
  64–5
amethysts 154–5
Ancient & Medieval
  Decorative Art,
  exhibition 11
Angell, J. & J. *80*
Arkwright, Sir Richard 44
armchair *34*
Art at Home 105
Art Nouveau 18, 19
  pewterware 86
Art of Beauty, The 31
Arthurian legends 8, 9
Arts & Crafts Exhibition
  Society 18
Ashbee, C. R., quoted 28
Ashworth, Geo. & Bros. 69
astronomy 149
Austria 7
  ceramics 60–1
  jewellery 150
  toys 135, 137
automata *see* clockwork
  toys
Ayrshire
  decorative objects 125
  textiles 44–5, 46

B

baby dolls 137–9
Baby's Opera, The, (W.
  Crane) *6*
Baccarat paperweight *103*
balloon-back chairs *23*, 32
bambooware, ceramics 67
Barry, Charles 8
Bassett-Lowke 141
Battam, Thomas 67, 102
Bavaria, toys 135–7
beaker, *transparentmalerei*
  101
Beattie, William 12
Beckford, William 8
bed-hangings 43–4
bedsteads 84
Belleek 63–4, *64*, 65
Belter, Henry 29
bentwood furniture 32, *33*
Berlin woolwork 44
Bessemer process 88–9
Bible boxes 120
Biedermeier 13, 14
  furniture 29, *32*
Bing, toys 141
Birmingham
  brass 83
  glass 100
bisque dolls *136–7*, 138
Blanchard, M. H., Son & Co.
  67
Blencow, Agnes 43
'Blue Perline' glass 107
blue-and-white tableware
  68–9
board games 134
Bohemian
  glass *98*, 99, *100, 102*
  porcelain 60–1
bone china 60, *61*, 66
books, childrens' 139
boot scraper *88*
Boston & Sandwich Glass
  Company 98, 102
boulle-work 120–1
Boulton, Matthew 85
Bow, ceramics 62
boxes *113*, *118–21*, *131*
  musical 134
bracelets *148–9*, 150,
  152–3
brass 83–4, *85*, *86*

decorative objects *118*,
  119, 120, 123
Brighton, Royal Pavilion 7
Bristol
  brass 83
  textiles 44
Britannia metal 86
broderie anglaise 46
bronze *78*, 84
brooches *147, 148, 150,
  152, 153, 154, 156*
Brown, Ford Madox 18
Bru, Leon Casimir & Son
  138
Brussels lace flounce *48*
building bricks *131*, 134
Burde & Abather 52
Burges, William 28
'Burmese' glass 106
Burne-Jones, Sir Edward 18
butterflies' wings 157

C

cabinet wares 62
Caldecott, Randolph 139
cameos *149, 150*, 151–2,
  155
  glass paperweight *103*
candelabra *78*
candlesticks 84, *86*
caneware, ceramics 67
card games 134
Carème 82
Carette 141
Carnival glass dish *106*
Carron Company 88
cased glass *96*, 100, *101, 102*
cashmere shawls 50
caskets *119*, 120
Cassell's Household Guide 32
  cast-iron objects *86, 88*
  furniture 86–9
  kitchenware 82–3
  toys *132*
Castellani, Fortunato Pio
  150, 155
catalogues 22, 23, 31
centrepiece, glass *107*
Century Vase 64
ceramics 58–75
Chair Maker's Guide, The 23
chairs
  balloon-back *23*, 24, 32

Bibliography

Aslin, Elizabeth *Nineteenth-Century English Furniture* (London, 1962)

Aslin, Elizabeth *The Aesthetic Movement* (London, 1969)

Barber, Edwin A. *The Pottery and Porcelain of the United States* (New York, 1893)

Cooper, Jeremy *Victorian and Edwardian Furniture and Interiors* (London, 1987)

Durant, Stuart *Victorian Ornamental Design* (London/New York, 1972)

Girouard, Mark *The Victorian Country House* (London, 1971)

Godden, Geoffrey A. *Victorian Porcelain* (London, 1961)

Hughes, G. Bernard *Antique Sheffield Plate* (London, 1970)

Jervis, Simon *High Victorian Design* (London, 1983)

Johnson, Marilynn, and others *19th-Century America: Furniture and Other Decorative Arts* (New York, 1970)

Joy, E.T. *Pictorial Dictionary of Nineteenth-Century Furniture Designs* (Woodbridge, 1977)

McClinton, Katherine M. *Collecting American Nineteenth-Century Silver* (New York, 1968)

McMorris, Penny *Crazy Quilts* (New York, 1984)

Manley, Cyril *Decorative Victorian Glass* (New York, 1981)

Morris, Barbara *Victorian Embroidery* (London/New York, 1962)

Morris, Barbara *Victorian Table Glass and Ornaments* (London, 1978)

Parry, Linda *William Morris Textiles* (London/New York, 1983)

Symonds, R.W., and Whinneray, B.B. *Victorian Furniture* (London, 1962)

Van Lemmen, Hans *Victorian Tiles* (Aylesbury, 1981)

Wakefield, Hugh *Nineteenth-Century British Glass* (London, 1961)

Wakefield, Hugh *Victorian Pottery* (London/New York, 1962)

Wardle, Patricia *Victorian Silver and Silver-plate* (London/New York 1963)

Wedgwood, Alexandra *A.W.N. Pugin and the Pugin Family* (London, 1985)

Wills, Geoffrey *Victorian Glass* (London, 1976)